The Anvil of
Guilt
and
Shame

A Man's Perspective on Abortion,
Forgiveness, and Calling

G. SPENCER SCHIRS JR.

ISBN 978-1-64670-666-2 (Paperback)
ISBN 978-1-64670-667-9 (Digital)

Covenant Books, Inc.
11661 Hwy 707
Murrells Inlet, SC 29576
www.covenantbooks.com

CONTENTS

INTRODUCTION

First and foremost, I thank God for the motivation to put my thoughts down. I have a message to men, especially those responsible for an *abortion*. Without Christ in my heart, I would not have the courage to speak to this truth. Sadly, God did not bless me with the ability to spell. I have struggled my whole life with spelling. I took classes and had tutors with very limited success. However, God blessed me with some of the most loving friends that willfully edited this book out of love and friendship.

I must thank several key people. First is my wife, Donna, my gift from God. She is my primary editor, sounding board, friend, and all the other great things that come from a Christ-first relationship. Then there is Mary P., the president of Right to Life from North Macomb County, Michigan, who guided me on this path, provided opportunities for me to speak, encouraged me, and became a great spiritual mentor and friend. Next are very dear friends, Kathryn and John who have become our brother and sisters in Christ. Our friendship began while serving on a ministry together. Over time, we became more like a family than just friends. Kathryn has also helped to edit this book and provided another women's point of view.

Then there are the guys—John, Jerry, Big Joe, Jim, and Ralph. God has blessed me with a small army of men who have shared life and encouraged me. They have provided spiritual guidance and direction with weekly accountability. These men are like brothers. Then there are three of my oldest friends—Charlie, Jim, and John—who always had my back. John laughed at me when I told him I wrote a book and pointed out I lack the ability to spell. He is right, however, he also encouraged and supported my efforts from that moment on. For over forty-five years, Charlie and John have laughed and cried with me, never giving up on me even when they should have. Then there is my Saturday morning group that Mr. Z and I started over ten years ago. We meet for coffee and share what is going on in our lives. We keep each other on God's path. We have the gruffly Marine Bob, Rob the Canadian, along with Dell who has been a disciple for over 75 years, (he camped with Moses) and of course there is Dan who always has a book for that! Many have passed through our group, but not a single man has ever left, not knowing that there are real men who love God.

I am blessed beyond words. I have asked these men to pray that this book will reach those who need something greater than what the world can offer (that is, every man on earth). Men who are seeking a brotherhood of *Godly* men who still make human errors but are willing to learn from their mistakes, leaving those mistakes at the cross, and then stand and support their brothers as they face their own issues.

> The Lord your God in your midst, The Mighty One, will save; He will rejoice over you with gladness, He will quiet you with His love, He will rejoice over you with singing. (Zephaniah 3:17 NKJV)

Men need to be a part of something. God wired us to be this way.

1

A Letter to My Child

As part of the process of coming to terms with "making a choice," an evolution of thought and action was required. One of the first actions was to express the internal emotions and begin a dialogue to the child I "chose" to kill at the altar of convenience. This is a letter to my child who I now call Grace.

The Lord's Grace to Paul

I thank Christ Jesus our Lord, who has given me strength, that he considered me trustworthy, appointing me to his service. Even though I was once a blasphemer and a persecutor and a violent man, I was shown mercy because I acted in ignorance and unbelief. The grace of our Lord was poured out on me abundantly, along with the faith and love that are in Christ Jesus.

Here is a trustworthy saying that deserves full acceptance: Christ Jesus came into the world to save sinners—of whom I am the worst. But for that very reason I was shown mercy so that in me, the worst of sinners, Christ Jesus might display his immense patience as an example for those

who would believe in him and receive eternal life.
Now to the King eternal, immortal, invisible, the
only God, be honor and glory for ever and ever.
Amen. (1 Timothy 1:12–17 NIV)

Where do I begin? I will never forget the look your mom had
that early summer day seeking for me to be a man. I am so sorry
I wasn't the man your mom needed me to be and how I failed to
be a man and fight for you. We bought the lies that you were simply a choice, nothing more than a cluster of cells to be sacrificed at
the altar of convenience. I apologize to you for not being the man I
thought I was. Because of my selfishness at that moment, I sacrificed
what was likely one of the greatest gifts I might ever receive—you.

I have imagined you as a little girl, for some reason, with big
eyes and an even bigger smile. Because of that image, there has been
an emptiness within me. A day has not passed that I do not think of
you and what my life would have been like with you in it. I imagine all we would have shared from your first steps to your first day
of school, comforting you on a stormy night, or even dealing with
teenage temper tantrums. Every time I hear a child laugh, I cannot
help but wonder what your laugh would have been like or what your
favorite flower or color might have been. Would you have liked cats
or dogs? Would you be a country girl or a city girl? All these questions go unanswered for now.

Your mom and I were young. Sadly, neither of us were grounded
in a relationship with Christ. That lack of spiritual guidance and clarity led me to making the choice of aborting you. I fully accept it was
my choice and failing. I alone am wholly responsible for the choice
that was made. Your mother was scared, and I failed as a man to give
her the support a real man would have. I believe that had I simply
asked her to keep you, she would have. The lie being sold on earth
that it is a woman's burden or health issue is just not true. It is a lie
right out of Satan's mouth. Truth is, you were written in God's book
of life, a life I cocreated and sadly erased.

God never gives up on us!

On earth, people come to God in many ways. Some are born into Christianity, others marry into it, and then you have lunkheads like me that need to lose everything to finally seek a relationship with Christ. I literally went blind and still denied Christ in my heart. I thought I could make it on my own if I just worked a little harder, a lie perpetuated by those measuring life by earthly standards, not Godly standards.

By 1999, I had undergone three years of eye surgeries and had regained most of my vision, yet I still chose to chase the earthly brass ring. The day came when I just wanted to quit! I remember it as though it was yesterday, ready to end my life on earth. One comforting thought I had was I knew I would finally get to meet you. Then a moment of clarity. I realized if I did get to see you, it would only be for a moment as I would most assuredly be heading to the furnace room. I can only imagine the beauty you see in heaven. Only knowing Christ without the experience of a broken world is in its own way a form of God's grace.

It took a few more years and a few more lumps; however, I finally started to seek Christ, partly motivated by the thought of being reunited with you. What is so amazing about how Christ works is he never gives up. Once you let him into your heart, he will chisel away at you until you are what he has always wanted you to become. Along with that transformation, he brought me my wife, Donna. She is so amazing! I know you would love her based on how I have seen her interact with the children she teaches about Christ. It is so much fun to see a little kid from church walk up to say hello to Ms. Donna. She is a gift from God to me. Please thank him for me!

Our spiritual walk has not always been on par. In the spring of 2005, she encouraged me to take part in a spiritual retreat called the "Walk to Emmaus." My reply was, "I will never retreat. I will only advance!" Well, because of her guidance and encouragement on April 7, 2005, I was taken to a church for three days of spiritual growth. Honestly, I didn't want to be there. I had earthly pursuits that needed my attention (so I thought). I even had an escape plan ready to put in action if I did not like what they were telling me! God put up a roadblock. As I walked in the church, there was a retired air force security police officer, a border patrol agent, and a judge who assured Donna that if I tried to leave, they would duct-tape me to a chair for the weekend! The first day and half was okay. I figured all these other guys need this, but I got this Christianity thing down. Oh, if it were only that simple! I was a new Christian, involved but not yet fully engaged. However, this was about to change.

On the morning of Saturday, April 9, 2005, one of the pastors gave a talk on the "means of grace." It became the most pivotal talk of the weekend for me. I learned of Christ's never-ending love and for-giveness. No matter how great my sin might have been, forgiveness was waiting if I would just accept Christ into my heart. As part of the talk, we were given the opportunity to accept Christ into our heart and surrender our burdens. I hesitated at first. Now I know it was because of you in my heart that I stood up and walked what seemed like a mile to the foot of the cross on that April morning.

As I approached the cross, the culmination of all the lies I told myself weighed heavily on me. That fifteen or twenty feet might as well have been twenty miles as all the memories rushed through my mind. I remembered the tear in your mother's eye as I handed her the money for the abortion. I saw the campfire where my friends assured me it wasn't my problem. Then I heard a whisper from God, encour-aging me to leave it at the cross. It was why I came. I felt the freedom of Christ overwhelming me. I knelt—but in truth, I collapsed at the cross with the full weight of my guilt and shame, pleading for Christ to take the pain of my "choice." I tried not to show my emotions, but I failed! As I wept, the men from my table surrounded me. I think they carried me back to my seat and prayed with me for the first time in an honest and loving way.

As the freedom of the redeeming love of Christ flowed over me, in that instant, an image of you smiling came over me. I knew in my heart you were okay and you are with Jesus. Satan lost another soul that day. Christ was about to turn my shame into a tool to fight Satan. You became my motivation. Because of you, I have a relation-ship with Christ through his prevenient grace. Because of the grace he has given me, I will forevermore call you Grace. You have had a profound effect on me, not as my earthly child, but as my heavenly advocate and personal angel.

Many times when I have been speaking on the topic of men and abortion, I have this image of sixty-three million babies murdered at the hand of Planned Parenthood, and they are praying for me. It is an amazing feeling when it comes over me and affirms that I am on the path God intended. To just bring one more man to God is a victory for Christ. The fight is now with the Satanic pro-choice advocates supporting genocide (abortion). Men have been removed from the conversation. Satan has masterfully used abortion as the tool to separate men from manhood. He also destroyed the black community, doing more damage than any other single factor. *How are they doing this?* Planned Parenthood, by design, is located in low income or predominantly black communities. Abortion is presented as a simple means out of a pregnancy. Satan has turned men into selfish, empty shells instead of what God intended them to be.

Satan has masterfully made abortion exclusively a woman's issue, removing the man and the child from the conversation, and they call it a women's health choice. Sadly, he is using the issue of abortion to destroy the traditional church here on earth. It must be so sad for Christ when he sees people making claims in his name that he would approve of abortion. Even worse is the lie that women, who have had an abortion, cannot go to heaven. It is just another lie for Satan to perpetuate. They call it compromise, but we know it is just Satan dividing people.

Even in tragedy, good can come. Grace, because of you, Christ is using me and has given me a mission to bring men into the conversion about abortion. I no longer fear Satan as I know in my heart that I am child of God, just as you are, and I have the love of Christ in my heart. Satan can no longer affect me. I have a freedom that only a Christian can fully understand. With this new freedom, I see the world with a different eye. I have to laugh at how Satan and his minions have gotten the secular world to think of Jesus as a 60s hippie. I will teach men the truth of Jesus and show them if they really want the world to see them as men, they need Christ in their heart. They can be forgiven of their sins, even abortion, if—and only if—they give their hearts and soul to Jesus and seek his forgiveness.

Before we meet in heaven, I will spend the remainder of my time enlightening every man and woman I can of how sinful abortion is and how supporting those that advocate for abortion is just as wrong. Christ has given me the scripture and the will to fight for you and all the other unborn children. I have an image of you in my mind. Now I know that when I leave this earth, we will finally be together. Oh, how it must be amazing to be face-to-face with Jesus. From the colors of heaven to being in the presence of Jesus Christ, it must be so amazing there!

Here on earth, there are a few songs that bring me to my knees every time I hear them because of you. When I hear "Happy Day" or "Where I Belong," I think of you and know I will be with you in heaven. You have my promise, Grace, that my every day will be focused on being able to hold your hand and meet Jesus, spending eternity with each of the aborted children that are assuredly in heaven. My dearest Grace, I love you. I always have, and I always will! God loves you, and so do I!

> Children are a heritage from the Lord, offspring a reward from him. Like arrows in the hands of a warrior are children born in one's youth. Blessed is the man whose quiver is full of them. They will not be put to shame when they contend with their opponents in court. (Psalm 127:3–5 NIV)

> Since, then, we know what it is to fear the Lord, we try to persuade others. What we are is plain to God, and I hope it is also plain to your conscience. We are not trying to commend ourselves to you again, but are giving you an opportunity to take pride in us, so that you can answer those who take pride in what is seen rather than in what is in the heart. If we are "out of our mind," as some say, it is for God; if we are in our right

mind, it is for you. For Christ's love compels us, because we are convinced that one died for all, and therefore all died. And he died for all, that those who live should no longer live for themselves but for him who died for them and was raised again.

So from now on we regard no one from a worldly point of view. Though we once regarded Christ in this way, we do so no longer. Therefore, if anyone is in Christ, the new creation has come: The old has gone, the new is here! All this is from God, who reconciled us to himself through Christ and gave us the ministry of reconciliation: that God was reconciling the world to himself in Christ, not counting people's sins against them. And he has committed to us the message of reconciliation. We are therefore Christ's ambassadors, as though God were making his appeal through us. We implore you on Christ's behalf: Be reconciled to God. God made him who had no sin to be sin for us, so that in him we might become the righteousness of God. (2 Corinthians 5:11–21 NIV)

The root meaning of the word *grace* comes from the Greek Charis, meaning "gift." Grace comes before our human decision or endeavors. We experience God's prevenient grace:

- through events, either positive or negative,
- through care and sacrifice of others (wives, girlfriends, etc.),
- through church and other believers,
- and through our words and actions.

2

Facing My Shame

God uses situations to provide us the opportunity to grow. How we respond is what determines whether we move closer to Christ or further away.

On April 9, 2005, as I knelt at the cross, I had been carrying the guilt and shame of the worst choice of my life, the abortion of my child, for twenty-four years. The pain I carried manifested in ways I can now see clearly because of Christ's redeeming love.

As I knelt, I felt cold and started shaking. In that very instance, I immediately recalled the early summer day when I met with Grace's mom and coldly handed her the money to abort our child. It was over for me, so I thought. I remember she was holding back the tears, biting her lip, and staying strong. Well, at least one of us was. She just said, "I'll take care of it." All it would have taken was me saying, "No, not our child!" The shame of not even being man enough to take her for the procedure illustrated what a self-centered, self-serving, and self-gratifying piece of human debris I was then. Thankfully, one of her girlfriends took her and provided her the comfort on my behalf. Shamefully, I wasn't even enough of a man to be by her side to deal with the aftermath that I created. No, I left her alone, only to gain the weight of guilt and shame of being the one responsible for the abortion of my child. Guilt comes from what I have done. Shame says this is who I am, and shame is from Satan.

Therefore we also, since we are surrounded by so great a cloud of witnesses, let us lay aside every weight, and the sin which so easily ensnares us, and let us run with endurance the race that is set before us, looking unto Jesus, the author and finisher of our faith, who for the joy that was set before Him endured the cross, despising the shame, and has sat down at the right hand of the throne of God. (Hebrews 12:1–2 NKJV)

The weight of abortion hung over me like an anvil every day, crushing my spirit. For the next twenty-four years, I was ashamed, avoiding love, commitment, and, frankly, responsibility for much of anything. Satan exploited my rift with Christ. He had free rein to use me as a tool for his wicked ways. He used my guilt, shame, and fear to drive me into darkness, which resulted in isolation from family and friends. I compensated with overindulgence in earthly pleasure with no regard to the eternal effect. It is a key point to how Satan operates. He preys on the vulnerable, the young, and especially the misinformed. He glamorizes decadence and immoral living. Satan has gleeful demons in media, entertainment, and politics, promoting secular living that is devoid of morals and heavenly directives.

True and False Disciples

Not everyone who says to me, "Lord, Lord," will enter the kingdom of heaven, but only the one who does the will of my Father who is in heaven. Many will say to me on that day, "Lord, Lord, did we not prophesy in your name and in your name drive out demons and in your name perform many miracles?" Then I will tell them plainly, "I never knew you. Away from me, you evildoers!" (Matthew 7:21–23 NIV)

Hell Is Real

To believe in heaven, you must also accept there is a hell. How could you not fear God saying he did not know you? Do you understand what this will mean to you? Try eternity in hell. There is no intervention once God passes judgment. There is no purgatory where your case is reviewed and decided. Every time I read Matthew 7:21–23, it resonates within me. Without reservation, I believe that Jesus came to earth to experience life among us and died for you and me, offering himself as a sacrifice for all our sins to provide a path for eternity, if we just allow him to be our Savior. Hell exists for God to deal righteously with Satan and, by extension, those who have chosen to do evil over good. Hell is real. Do you really want to spend eternity there?

On that April day in 2005, I took the first step on a long path of redemption with a special comfort of knowing I had my own special angel looking over me. When I wrote the letter to Grace, I wept. I still weep now because I know how incredibly selfish I was but more so what a god*less* waste I had become. However, by God's *grace*, I am forgiven. I will be reunited with my special angel, Grace. Because of Christ's redeeming love, I feel that maybe I might not go to hell.

> He will punish those who do not know God and do not obey the gospel of our Lord Jesus. They will be punished with everlasting destruction and shut out from the presence of the Lord and from the glory of his might. (2 Thessalonians 1:8–9 NIV)

God's love is so great. He is more than capable of forgiving all our sins. However, asking for his forgiveness is not a "get out of hell" free card. Simply being a good person does not get you into heaven. There are definable steps required. It is only a starting point of the rest of your life. A life in Christ is the greatest challenge and most rewarding action you will ever undertake.

Shame Stifled Me

Earthly pleasure can never replace what God desires for us; shame keeps me from God, putting earthly objective over faith. I collected people—in a sense, women—as trophies. They were my conquests, my game. When I saw a woman who interested me, I pursued her until I established a relationship with my objective simply being sex and nothing else. I did not care about her feelings, dreams, or desires. They were simply a notch in the bedpost. I was such a jerk that once I accomplished my primary goal, I moved on to the next. Yes, I was that guy! It was easy. It allowed me the freedom to do what I wanted at the expense of the very people I should have allowed into my life. Secularism is sexy. If there is no God, then there is no reason for morality. Live as you please and indulge in whatever brings pleasure.

You would think the shame of being responsible for an abortion would have men on their knees, begging for God's forgiveness. However, Satan uses guilt and shame to accomplish his goal of removing men from the equation and skillfully creating a narrative that abortion is a women's health issue and no concern of men. I have often wondered—and there is no way to confirm this—how many of the sixty-three million abortions since the *Roe v. Wade* decision of 1973 have resulted in men spending their lives numbing themselves to the guilt and shame by:

- becoming a workaholic,
- using alcohol to hide the pain, resulting in becoming an alcoholic,
- isolating themselves, removed from life and family,
- being addicted to drugs,
- contemplating suicide or displaying behaviors like moodiness and selfishness,
- and treating women as objects rather than the partner God intended.

These *hurts, habits,* or *hang-ups* destroy men, driving them away from a relationship with God and a healthy meaningful relationship with others, especially with the very women they impregnated! Now I get that abortion has a physical, emotional, and psychological effect on women. They were trusted by God with the womb. I can never fully understand the women's feelings, however, do not think that abortion has no effect on men. It is a lie direct from Satan, and those that propagate that lie are doing Satan's work.

History is going to show that one of the greatest lies ever told was that a baby is simply a choice and that abortion is exclusively a women's issue. Every abortion is Satan's victory. Every time a man is removed from the decision or refused having a family is a victory for Satan. Each one of the sixty-three million abortions from 1973 mean there are the same number of men absolved of responsibility. Again, this is a victory for Satan. He is using this issue because he removes a man from the role that which God calls him. Satan drives three more souls into darkness.

- God equipped women with a womb. I did not appreciate this until I learned what a woman goes through during pregnancy. Men are not tough enough for childbirth. Just imagine a golf ball passing through your penis.
- The man is called to be a leader and a father.
- Most importantly, a child, has been erased from God's book of life.

Contrary to the pro-choice position, no abortion needs to occur. They will counter with, "What about rape or incest?" Truth be told, those small percentage of abortions are negligible. What credibility can an organization that kills babies then harvests their organs to sell them have? What kind of man stands by and allows this to happen? Not a real man with Christ living within his heart.

3

Never Forget the Women

Life in God's Garden

The Lord God planted a garden eastward in Eden, and there He put the man whom He had formed. And out of the ground the Lord God made every tree grow that is pleasant to the sight and good for food. The tree of life was also in the midst of the garden, and the tree of the knowledge of good and evil. Now a river went out of Eden to water the garden, and from there it parted and became four riverheads. The name of the first is Pishon; it is the one which skirts the whole land of Havilah, where there is gold. And the gold of that land is good. Bdellium and the onyx stone are there. The name of the second river is Gihon; it is the one which goes around the whole land of Cush. The name of the third river is Hiddekel; it is the one which goes toward the east of Assyria. The fourth river is the Euphrates. Then the Lord God took the man and put him in the garden of Eden to [e]tend and keep it. And the Lord God commanded the man, saying, "Of every tree of the garden you may freely eat; but of the tree of the knowledge of good and evil you shall not eat, for in the day that you eat of it you shall surely die." And the Lord God said, "It is not good that man should be alone; I will make him a helper comparable to him." Out of the ground the Lord God formed every beast of the field and every bird of the air, and brought them to Adam to see what he would call them. And whatever Adam called each living creature, that was its name. So Adam gave names to all cattle, to the birds of the air, and to every beast of the field. But for Adam there was not found a helper comparable to him. And the Lord God caused a deep sleep to fall on Adam, and he slept; and He took one of his ribs, and closed up the flesh in its place. Then the rib which the Lord God had taken from man He made into a woman, and He brought her to the man. And Adam said:

"This is now bone of my bones And flesh of my flesh; She shall be called Woman, Because she was taken out of Man."

Therefore a man shall leave his father and mother and be joined to his wife, and they shall become one flesh. And they were both naked, the man and his wife, and were not ashamed. (Genesis 2:8–25 NKJV)

From the very beginning, God meant for men and women to be together. God created women to be helpmates for men, not servants. Do not confuse this as the pathological misleaders of the secular, liberal progressivism have done.

For over fifty years now, there has been an effort to empower women by creating a lie that women do not need men. They lie to women at every turn, creating false images of what women should or need to be, how they should look and act, or how they should interact with men. They use imagery to brainwash young women into believing that true happiness is found through clothing, zip code, or social status. Every other commercial is related to either weight loss or beauty products. A "modern woman" is expected to be beautiful at all times with makeup and within three ounces of what she weighed when she was married (if she chose such an antiquated method). A modern woman is expected to have a full-time career while raising healthy, well-adjusted, and responsible children (a man being optional). This same woman carries the burden of maintaining her independence while having time for herself, and do it all without the encumbrance of a man.

In truth, all the secular world really has to offer is both earthly emptiness and eternal risk.

Here, again, the cancer of secular, liberal progressivism has destroyed the man's value while brainwashing women into the false teaching that earthly accomplishment have more value than God's intent. The entertainment industry have also portrayed men as incapable of functioning without the guidance of an even stronger woman. What is truly ironic is that the secular, liberal will defend the Muslim faith than chastises Christianity while ignoring the truth of how Muslim women are treated. Christianity, if taught truthfully, glorify women and celebrate their importance. Yet the liberal progressives, with their co-conspirators in media and entertainment, dismiss and denigrate God.

Now allow me to be clear, there is nothing wrong with independent, confident women. However, in the lie of the secular, liberal progressive, the man is just an option, not necessary for a great life. Women are absolutely amazing. Real men recognize and celebrate it. Men are not nearly tough enough to give birth to new life or nurture a child as God intended. However, do not buy the lie that a man is not necessary in the home or in raising children.

The belief that women do not need men is an ungodly lie that secular liberalism have used to separate women from men. The world will even suggest that having children makes her less of a woman because they should have a career over what God intended them for. Women have been manipulated into waiting to have children until after they have established their career. If they unfortunately get pregnant, they are told not to worry because an abortion is their way out. Of course, they never shared the health and emotional risks. The part they fail to tell them is the decreased likelihood of finding a meaningful relationship, having a healthy child, or the health effects on women as they get older.

The Unspoken Health Effects

Another consideration they refuse to talk about—breast cancer is linked to abortion and the birth control pill. In a book by Dr. Chris Kahlenborn, based on a six-year study and a meticulous analysis of hundreds of scientific documents, he talks about the effect that abortion and hormonal contraception have on breast, uterine, cervical, liver, and other cancers.

I spoke of the lies that are perpetuated regarding abortion. Again, this lie is propagated and echoed by the media and entertainment. In truth, if women's health was the concern, then why are they not sharing that the suicide rate increases in women after an abortion or that a woman may experience a lifelong feeling of emptiness and heartache over the choice.

One study conducted in Finland shows a three times greater risk of suicide and another indicates a thirty-seven-percent increase. A simple Google search can provide countless studies. Yet it still begs the question, if abortion has even a one percent correlation with suicide, then isn't suicide a preventable health issue? Why then are the genocidal maniacs at Planned Parenthood not telling women, especially young women, that they are going to potentially suffer from lifelong depression and are placing themselves at an increased likelihood of cancer, depression, and suicidal thoughts?

> There are six things the Lord hates, seven that are detestable to him: haughty eyes, a lying tongue, hands that shed innocent blood, a heart that devises wicked schemes, feet that are quick to rush into evil, a false witness who pours out lies

and a person who stirs up conflict in the community. (Proverbs 6:16–19 NIV)

The liberal progressives have masterfully manipulated truth and led women by partial truths and lies. I would go as far as to say that the only one more masterful in mass manipulation was Joseph Goebbles, Adolf Hitler's propaganda minister. If you look objectively at their goals, the liberal progressives are just as evil.

4

Misinformation

Misinformation is the tool of Satan himself. He uses it to manipulate people into false beliefs, teachings, and lifestyles. Satan also uses scripture. Some of the most evil are the most scripturally versed people you will ever meet.

> Woe to those who call evil good and good evil,
> who put darkness for light and light for darkness,
> who put bitter for sweet and sweet for bitter.
> (Isaiah 5:20 NIV)

I personally know and have directly interacted with a pastor who uses title and position along with partial Scripture to advocate for a non-biblical cause—a cause of emotion and feeling devoid of scriptural support. I will be the first to stand and defend a person's right to fight for what they believe in, however, when a pastor uses position in an intentional, non-scriptural way, it is demonstrably wrong. It is false teaching, and God addresses that. God also speaks to misusing his word.

A word of warning, when people use a sentence of scripture, never hesitate to ask what else the chapter says then read it yourself! *Scripture is often misused and misquoted. The only way to avoid falling into this trap is to read the Bible yourself!* The Bible is available to all, not just priests and pastors. An unread Bible in the bookcase is not a hedge of protection that gets you into heaven, but there are more than a few people who think it is. One scripture, likely the most recognized, is John 3:16. Christians throw it around rarely following it up. What about John 3:17–18?

> For God did not send His Son into the world to condemn the world, but that the world through Him might be saved. "He who believes in Him is not condemned; but he who does not believe is condemned already, because he has not believed in the name of the only begotten Son of God." (John 3:17–18 NKJV)

Proceed with extreme caution. Opening and reading the Bible will potentially change everything for you. Face it, your way is not working! That voice is of the Holy Spirit wooing you. It is time to let go. God loves you, and there is nothing you can do to stop him!

> But without faith *it is* impossible to please *Him*, for he who comes to God must believe that He is, and *that* He is a rewarder of those who diligently seek Him. (Heb 11:6 NKJV)

Like most, I lived for many years in the belief that I was unworthy of Christ's love because of several experiences. The first was a misquoted and misunderstood scripture I hung my faith on. For years, I felt doomed because on one occasion, a man who touted himself as a Christian, misquoted one scripture and burdened me with a lie. I was told that I carried the burden of my father's sin, quoting Exodus 34:7.

> Yet he does not leave the guilty unpunished; he punishes the children and their children for the sin of the parents to the third and fourth generation. (Exodus 34:7 NIV)

This scripture was used like a threat, creating burden and uncertainty. Scripture without direction and guidance is like handing a loaded gun to a child, expecting them to understand the potential impact, and trusting that they'll simply figure it out! It was out of context. The man who had issues with my father used it as a way—I think, in his mind—to get at my father. I did not speak to my father about it until months before his death. When I told him what happened, he began to cry, assuring me it wasn't true. He expressed his remorse of not teaching me more about the love of God. I allowed this misquote to destroy my spirit. Why didn't I speak to him about it? Why did I keep it to myself? Sadly, this would be one of the last meaningfully conversations my father and I had before he succumb to his battle with cancer. My father died before I gave my heart to Christ. I wish he and I could have walked this path together. I hope that if you are a man on this path, you teach your sons and daughters of Christ's love. It will change their lives in immeasurable ways. If communicated incorrectly, scripture can be a weapon of destruction, crushing a person's soul.

The second experience related to me being unworthy of Christ's love. A "good Catholic family" that might have been great Catholics but horrible Christians! At that point in my life, I was seeking answers, but because I was not of the Catholic religion, I could not be a member of their pack. They held their religion out as being special, as though it made them better than others. The family appearance took priority over being disciples of Christ. The father and mother would use bits of scripture to point out the failings of others. Since I did not measure up to their religious standard, it was made clear that I was not worthy of their tribe. Rather than following what God tells us in scripture, they simply turned their back on the lost (me).

A real Christian man would have taken that opportunity to mentor and teach. A real Christian man would have trained his sons to guide and mentor the lost, not judge them unworthy based on religious alliance. A true Christian woman would have used her God-given nurturing to bring the lost into the Christian fold. Sadly, one of the most common reasons people walk away from the church and faith is falling victim to scriptural misinformation. If the people of the church mindfully misuse scripture to keep people away from either their family or friends, then they are falling way short of God's expectations! God knows and sees the hypocrisy. And when the judgement day comes, will your heart and actions align with your church persona or your real persona? Misquoting scripture to manipulate or harm people to false teaching is the work of Satan himself, and a standard tool of the secular world. It has only one purpose: to separate people from God.

Buying into Scriptural Falsehoods

Again, I must stress the importance of biblical study and seeking strong mentors to help you on your journey. *Do not try to go at it alone.* You are like the gazelle, separated from the herd. The lion is Satan, and he is going to attack. Your scriptural truth will take time and discernment. Do not go at it alone. It will kill your spirit.

It took time for me to come to terms with all the lies I was fed. It also took time to come to terms with my relationship with my earthly father. Once I understood the scriptural truth of my sins versus my father's sins, I was free to live my life to glorify God. I was finally able to resolve that both my father and I will stand before God for his final judgment. *No one* on earth can intercede for either of us.

That conversation is exclusive to you and God. God will only ask you two questions, and how you answer them is what will determine your eternal life. I will not share the questions because it requires studying scripture to learn that truth! There are so many false teachers who tell you that your works get you into heaven or your church involvement, but they are wrong. Now understand that God has many expectations of us. Works are part of it, however, your works alone will not get you into heaven. Being a good person will not balance out your other sins. Using your talent without praising God for that gift can quickly give you an earthly belief of being special. Talent is a God-given gift. Using that gift to glorify God is your true mission. However, most of us are not taught this so we fall into secular lies and misdirection.

The Bible is such an amazing book. A trusted mentor once told me, "What is the acronym for Bible? Basic Instructions Before Leaving Earth!" I love that! As my journey continues, the BIBLE acronym has come to life.

As you walk this path, the closer you get to Christ, the more real the Bible will become, and the clarity will amaze you! The events of the world will give you a clarity that you can only fully understand in conjunction with a scriptural basis. Don't buy their lies! The problems of the world today have so much to do with the lies and misinformation perpetuated willfully by liberal progressives with the aid of the demonic accomplices in the media and entertainment industries.

Scripture is God's living word, and men need the strength and guidance available in scripture. However, the liberals fear you knowing this truth. This truth would expose them as idolaters of earthly idols. God calls us to live in the *world*, *not* to be of the *world*.

A very wise and trusted man once said to me, "How dare you hang your head in shame and live under the misguided belief that you are not worthy of God's forgiveness?" He sent his son for you, and Jesus, willfully took the sin of the *world* to the cross. He created a path for you to heaven. What kind of idiots filled your head with such misguided beliefs?

5

So Where Is the Church?

If my people, who are called by my name, will humble
themselves and pray and seek my face and turn from
their wicked ways, then I will hear from heaven, and
I will forgive their sin and will heal their land.
—2 Chron. 7:14 NIV

So where is the church? You would think that an issue such as
abortion would unite the people or the church. Instead, the church
cowers in the corner, afraid of offending someone. The liberals have
successfully muzzled priests and pastors from standing on scriptural
truths. The fear of earthly consequence and possibly offending someone has become a greater fear than the scriptural truth of answer-
ing to God! As a result, the weak and Sunday-only Christians have
turned their back on the issue of abortion, being misled to false teachings. This weakness has festered for decades and led to the church of
compromise.

The Church of Compromise

The question then becomes, do these "churches of compromise" really believe in God? Do they really believe God sent his only
son to live among us and to take the sin of the world to the cross?

Do they really believe that the only path to heaven is through Jesus Christ or are they just simply faking their faith to earthly ends? Do not kid yourself; this is by design. The church has been infested by the well-meaning people that put more concern in meaningless secularism and feelings than the truth of God. We are called to love, however, we are not called to compromise on God's teachings. They have.

Compromise would say yes to all no matter how absurd they may be. There is nothing scripturally to say otherwise. To an authentic Christian, God is real and the Bible is his inspired word. Within the church of compromise, the Bible is a moving target that should evolve to today's issues. The Bible is either the truth or just a book of stories in the compromise world. Feelings and opinions have more meaning. Compromise would allow for flexible interpretation of the Bible, allowing meanings to fit the emotions of the day. Clearly, I fall in the camp that the Bible is the inspired word of God. I am not equipped to challenge God on his word or willing to risk eternity in a lake of fire. The more I read the Bible, the more alive it becomes, and the application to the events of the day are more clear.

Compromise is a cancer to truth. It will lead to the slow and ugly death of the church, just like the RMS *Titanic* hitting the iceberg. It is playing out exemplified by the abortion and gay marriage issue currently facing many denominations.

On June 1, 2019, at the Michigan United Methodist Church Annual Conference, a motion to recognize the *unborn baby* as fully human was voted down.

The Great White Throne Judgment

Then I saw a great white throne and Him who sat on it, from whose face the earth and the heaven fled away. And there was found no place for them. And I saw the dead, small and great, standing before God, and books were opened. And another book was opened, which is the Book of Life. And the dead were judged according to their works, by the

things which were written in the books. The sea
gave up the dead who were in it, and Death and
Hades delivered up the dead who were in them.
And they were judged, each one according to his
works. Then Death and Hades were cast into the
lake of fire. This is the second death. And anyone
not found written in the Book of Life was cast into
the lake of fire. (Revelation 20:11–15 NKJV)

These delegates have crossed a line of pure evil. The vote came
down to: affirm or yes at 426 and opposed or no at 597. Satan's own
597 have infiltrated the United Methodist Church and have acted by
their vote. These demons of Satan will stand in God's judgment. I
pray they come back to scriptural truth before they stand before him
or they better like it extremely hot. The United Methodist Church
is on the highway to hell! It saddens me as it was where I began my
faith walk, but the cancer of secular progressivism has overtaken the
denomination. The United Methodist Church will eventually split
between traditional values and the current idea of the hippie-dippie,
good time, feel goodism that is infecting a faction of the church.
This is a little different, than it once did over the issue of slavery.
Assuredly, the progressives will say they would side with abolition,
but facts just don't support that argument. It was the compromisers
that wanted to allow churches to decide if they were for or against
slavery. They didn't want to offend anyone!

History repeats itself. These compromisers have lost the way of
scriptural truth. They will pay an eternal price for their sin. The argument is always the same. "I feel it isn't fair" or "What would Jesus
do?" Seriously, they ask what would Jesus do. The simple answer is
to read the scripture. They'll immediately respond with, "Times are
different." This is a hollow argument. If you read the Bible, you will
quickly discover its timelessness. However, they want the Bible to
change to their will. They "feel" it is only fair that men can marry
men and women can marry women. Where does this stop? Should
men be allowed to marry sheep or dogs? Should a woman who loves
cats be allowed to marry her cat in church?

My fight is regarding abortion!

My fight is not with the gay community. My fight is about abortion. Sadly, the two issues have been blended within the church to involve the emotional response of the scripturally weak. So the very same people fighting for gay rights are generally the same people justifying abortion as a women issue or, in the case of the United Methodist Church, voting that a baby is not fully human.

With the cancer-like growth of the secular movement within the church, the church has lost its moral high ground. With the festering growth of political correctness, truth cannot be freely spoken without first being edited to ensure it is inoffensive. Sadly, Satan is killing the church from a death of a thousand cuts. People have walked away not because of God, but because of the lack of real men who are standing up for what is right. Misguided men and women have misinterpreted God's word. Some did it by intent! Satan is doing a happy dance with the conflicted within the church. The division feeds and sadly provides Satan strength by confusing people into to believing false truths. More division within the church will not end well for those who choose the path of compromise. In Isaiah, God foretells of how he feels. As followers of Christ we have a responsibility to warn our families, coworkers, and friends, they do however have free will.

> Woe to those who call evil good and good evil;
> Who put darkness for light, and light for darkness, Who put bitter for sweet, and sweet for bitter. (Is 5:20 NKJV)

Compromise Is the Work of Satan

In the church of compromise, abortion is accepted and considered normal, which is *a false teaching*. The churches that are promoting false teachings will have to answer to God for eternity.

False Teachers and Their Destruction

But there were also false prophets among the people, just as there will be false teachers among you. They will secretly introduce destructive heresies, even denying the sovereign Lord who bought them—bringing swift destruction on themselves. Many will follow their depraved conduct and will bring the way of truth into disrepute. In their greed these teachers will exploit you with fabricated stories. Their condemnation has long been hanging over them, and their destruction has not been sleeping.

For if God did not spare angels when they sinned, but sent them to hell, putting them in chains of darkness[b] to be held for judgment; if he did not spare the ancient world when he brought the flood on its ungodly people, but protected Noah, a preacher of righteousness, and seven others; if he condemned the cities of Sodom and Gomorrah by burning them to ashes, and made them an example of what is going to happen to the ungodly; and if he rescued Lot, a righteous man, who was distressed by the depraved conduct of the lawless (for that righteous man, living among them day after day, was tormented in his righteous soul by the lawless deeds he saw and heard)—if this is so, then the Lord knows how to rescue the godly from trials and to hold the unrighteous for punishment on the day of judgment. This is especially true of those who follow the corrupt desire of the flesh and despise authority. Bold and arrogant, they are not afraid to heap abuse on celestial beings; yet even angels, although they are stronger and more powerful, do not heap abuse on such beings when bringing judgment on them from the Lord. But these people blaspheme in matters they do not understand. They are like unreasoning animals, creatures of instinct, born only to be caught and destroyed, and like animals they too will perish. They will be paid back with harm for the harm they have done. Their idea of pleasure is to carouse in broad daylight. They are blots and blemishes, reveling in their pleasures while they feast with you. With eyes full of adultery, they never stop sinning; they seduce the unstable; they are experts in greed—an accursed brood! They have left the straight way and wandered off to follow the way of Balaam son of Bezer, who loved the wages of wickedness. But he was rebuked for his wrongdoing by a donkey—an animal without speech—who spoke with a human voice and restrained the prophet's madness.

These people are springs without water and mists driven by a storm. Blackest darkness is reserved for them. For they mouth empty, boastful words and, by appealing to the lustful desires of the flesh, they entice people who are just escaping from those who live in error. They promise them freedom, while they themselves are slaves of depravity—for "people are slaves to whatever has mastered them." If they have escaped the corruption of the world by knowing our Lord and Savior Jesus Christ and are again entangled in it and are overcome, they are worse off at the end than they were at the beginning. It would have been better for them not to have known the way of righteousness, than to have known it and then to turn their backs on the sacred command that was passed on to them. Of them the proverbs are true: "A dog returns to its vomit," and, "A sow that is washed returns to her wallowing in the mud." (2 Peter 2:1–22 NIV)

It saddens me to observe what is going on within the church and that so many men have stepped away to allow the enemy to influence their minds, destroy families, and weaken people. Don't compromise, if only it were so easy. God never promised us that life on earth will be easy. In life, we are often faced with hard, life-altering decisions.

The church policy should simply be, if you are pro-choice, you are pro-murder and should repent. They should go even further and not allow those people or their families to enter the church out of reverence for God.

Well, let's get political!

How can any Democrat or RINO Republican show their faces at church? The time has come for the church to come home to scriptural truth and deal with the events that will result. The *truth* of the matter is; when pro-choice politicians show their faces in church it is to get votes. If they knew Christ and honestly followed him or had an ounce of integrity, how possibly would they dare enter a church? Sadly, the gullible will vote for them, because they saw them in church. Imagine if a politician sat in the front, and the priest or pastor pointed them out for supporting the murder of children, and asked the real men of God to remove them!

Church would get interesting!

Here is why I am not part of church leadership. Within the Catholic church, they should excommunicate any and all Catholics that support abortion. No compromise, Hail Marys, or penance, just a boot in the ass to the door! The same approach to sexual misconduct would show the world that the church is of God, not of the world! God will not compromise on his truth, so shouldn't the church have a zero-compromise policy to secular attitudes? Within the Protestant church, membership and association should be stripped from those involved in either sexual misconduct or pro-choice (baby murder) advocacy.

You cannot call yourself a Christian and support *murdering babies*. Period. As a believer, we are all in God's Book of Life. I don't think erasing the names of the unborn will ingratiate you with God. All I can do is pray for you. Additionally, the church should pay for all psychological therapy and medical expenses for the victims of the sexual misconduct by priest or pastors as well as all the legal fees for the victims and their families. The church should disallow any politician who is pro-choice from membership or association. The greater church is in peril and requires real action before Satan has the victory he seeks. A weakened church is where self-identified Christians walk away rather than stand for scriptural truth.

Above all: Return to teaching the truth of Christ and stop teaching he was a 60's hippie!

6

If the Church Only Fought Back

On January 23, 2019, the Vatican and Pope Francis had an opportunity to take the first step in redeeming itself for Christ and living up to God's expectations. Imagine the effect of a strong church that refuses to compromise on faith, scripture, morals, and truth, a church bold enough to remove the welcome mat for the abortionist, pedophiles, and those that support them.

On this date, New York governor, Andrew Cuomo signed the Reproductive Health Act—in truth, the "baby murder act"—and flagrantly celebrated the pro-abortion bill. The bill allows the outright murder of babies in the third term and even after they are born alive. Cuomo stated that it was "a historic victory for New Yorkers and our progressive values."

Progressivism and Christianity do not mix. It is the difference of good and evil.

Cuomo has touted his Roman Catholic faith and the fact that he was a former altar boy in his state address. He used his association with the Catholic church to advance his political career and the murder of children. He is not a godly man. The Pope and Vatican should have excommunicated Governor Cuomo within a minute of him signing the bill and admonish the governor to never identify himself as a Catholic.

The Pope, Vatican, and Catholicism would have started on a path of restoration, establishing to worldly men that the church is a no-nonsense house of faith to God. Catholicism would have earned back a piece of the respect they once held, and many seeking guidance might well have felt drawn back to the Catholic church.

Meanwhile in Virginia, one of Satan's demons, Democratic delegate Kathy Tran sponsored the Repeal Act, which seeks to repeal restrictions on third-trimester abortions that carried the support of top Democrats in the state, including Governor Ralph Northam. These purely evil people are doing Satan's work, which the church should call them out for.

If the church leads, people will follow.

In California, it has been reported that late-term babies have been aborted to harvest their organs—such as the heart, liver, pancreas, kidneys, and even their brain. Where is the church? This is a genocide greater than anything ever experienced. The Catholic church held a "Nine Days For Life" prayer vigil! Why is it not every day for life? I am certain that God is pro-life and would doubt he only thinks of babies when an event rolls around.

The church has failed God when it comes to the issue of abortion.

Less We Forget How Great We Once Were

Here is a truth that will make the liberals cringe. There are zero institutions of higher learning built by great secularists, liberals, or progressives. They do not exist because there is no such thing! However, the same cannot be said about the church, especially the Catholic church. I am not Catholic! But if people bothered to look at history, they might discover most universities were established by churches, institutions like Harvard (1636) and Yale (1701) were originally established for the education of ministers, not whiny, liberal brats. The College of Philadelphia (known today as the University of

Pennsylvania) as well as the University of Delaware were established by Benjamin Franklin assisted by Reverend Alison, neither secular liberals.

The greatness of the church was what supported building this country. Most community hospitals were also the creation of the church, *not the government!* No progressive professors have ever established a college or university, let alone built a single hospital. No, it was the church. News flash, the church is not the building on the corner. It is the people within it, people who work to glorify God on earth as it is in heaven. The community church fed and housed the homeless, sheltered unwed mothers, and facilitated the adoption of unplanned children. They had convents all over the country, and the majority had a section set aside for unwed mothers where they could give birth and then put their child up for adoption. But because the passive church allowed the cancer of secularism, liberalism, and progressivism to grow out of control, the Christian-centered community is at risk, including the role of man. The church could be revived if, and only if, the people of the church take a hard stand of being the unwavering moral center, starting by teaching boys how to become real men.

So a personal plea, come to church and learn of the truth of God. What harm could come from enriching people, sharing our lives with others, and seeking the truth. If I am wrong, it will not hurt you. If I am wrong, all you have lost is a little time or a Facebook or Instagram post. However, if you're wrong…well, eternity is a long time!

Before You Jump In

Do not volunteer for anything until you are firm in your faith. Clarification, *do not* volunteer for any committee addressing church business no matter how qualified you are. That is the fastest way to lose faith. Nothing will drain your spirit faster than sitting on the finance committee, steering committee, or outreach committee. Just don't do it. There will be a time for it later.

I mistakenly joined an outreach committee at the request of the pastor. She pulled me aside and told me how my experience in sales and marketing would be invaluable. So I said okay! I was not ready to deal with some of the narrow-mindedness of the other people on the committee. For most, it was simply a social group. When we spoke about outreach and church marketing, it was like a high school marketing class. I met with the pastor and expressed my frustration. She and I ended up having a secret marketing committee where we came up with the ideas that she presented to the group as hers. The others in the group, wanting to please her, simply followed her lead.

Now you may feel called to serve as a leader. I just caution you to first focus on your spiritual growth before you take on the burden of church politics. Engage in small groups and Bible studies first, learn and grow.

How We Got to This Point

Prior to WWII, the church was the center of the neighborhood and the community. Everyone from a given neighborhood was there. The kids were all together, and the parents had community. At the center of that community was the priest or pastor of the church. He was the primary mediator, counselor, and a voice of reason. The children knew they could turn to him, especially if there were issues at home. The pastor or priest would intervene by a casual offer of coffee or inviting himself to dinner. He would interject himself into a family and provide loving counsel. They were the peacekeepers of the neighborhood, the arbitrator, and often the adjudicator.

Satan was working to make the church lack relevancy. The stage was set in the post-world war. Men had seen evil and now just wanted peace in their home and life. The post-war children, the baby boomers (1945–1964) enjoyed more freedom than every generation before it. Families had more time and freedom than ever. A recipe for compromise was set to water down Christ as less than relevant in the post-war world, and Satan was in the kitchen. Satan and his progressive minions turned Jesus into a hippie.

7

Jesus Was Not a 60s Hippie

The phrase "what would Jesus do" has been framed to make Jesus into a passive middle-of-the road wimp! It's the church's battle cry! There is nothing to support this idea of Jesus being an indecisive liberal. His every word was measured and truthful. It was guiding and insightful. If we bought the secular Christian belief that Jesus was a 60's hippie, it would all make sense.

What a load of non-scripturally supported crap!

> He will punish those who do not know God and do not obey the gospel of our Lord Jesus. They will be punished with everlasting destruction and shut out from the presence of the Lord and from the glory of his might. (2 Thessalonians 1:8–9 NIV)

If the idea of hippie Jesus were remotely true, then the lie would justify the denial of morality, culpability, integrity, and common sense! Jesus was anything but a hippie. Christianity and the issue of abortion (murdering babies) all stem from this misguided idea that Jesus was a passive wimp! It is just not the truth. The church lost its relevancy and chose to step back rather than step forward. Sadly, a lot of hippies went into ministry and identified with hippie Jesus so they propitiated that lie. When Jesus returns, he will not come as a stinking hippie. He will be returning to dispense the justice of God.

> Jude, a servant of Jesus Christ and a brother of James, To those who have been called, who are loved in God the Father and kept for Jesus Christ: Mercy, peace and love be yours in abundance.

The Sin and Doom of Ungodly People

Dear friends, although I was very eager to write to you about the salvation we share, I felt compelled to write and urge you to contend for the faith that was once for all entrusted to God's holy people. For certain individuals whose condemnation was written about long ago have secretly slipped in among you. They are ungodly people, who pervert the grace of our God into a license for immorality and deny Jesus Christ our only Sovereign and Lord. Though you already know all this, I want to remind you that the Lord at one time delivered his people out of Egypt, but later destroyed those who did not believe. And the angels who did not keep their positions of authority but abandoned their proper dwelling—these he has kept in darkness, bound with everlasting chains for judgment on the great Day. In a similar way, Sodom and Gomorrah and the surrounding towns gave themselves up to sexual immorality and perversion. They serve as an example of those who suffer the punishment of eternal fire. In the very same way, on the strength of their dreams these ungodly people pollute their own bodies, reject authority and heap abuse on celestial beings. But even the archangel Michael, when he was disputing with the devil about the body of Moses, did not himself dare to condemn him for slander but said, "The Lord rebuke you!" Yet these people slander whatever they do not understand, and the very things they do understand by instinct—as irrational animals do—will destroy them. Woe to them! They have taken the way of Cain; they have rushed for profit into Balaam's error; they have been destroyed in Korah's rebellion. These people are blemishes at your love feasts, eating with you without the slightest qualm—shepherds who feed only themselves. They are clouds without rain, blown along by the wind; autumn trees, without fruit and uprooted—twice dead. They are wild waves of the sea, foaming up their shame; wandering stars, for whom blackest darkness has been reserved forever. Enoch, the seventh from Adam, prophesied about them: "See, the Lord is coming with thousands upon thousands of his holy ones to judge everyone, and to convict all of them of all the ungodly acts they have committed in their ungodliness, and of all the defiant words ungodly sinners have spoken against him." These people are grumblers and faultfinders; they follow their own evil desires; they boast about themselves and flatter others for their own advantage.

A Call to Persevere

But, dear friends, remember what the apostles of our Lord Jesus Christ foretold. They said to you, "In the last times there will be scoffers who will follow their own ungodly desires." These are the people who divide you, who follow mere natural instincts and do not have the Spirit.

But you, dear friends, by building yourselves up in your most holy faith and praying in the Holy Spirit, keep yourselves in God's love as you wait for the mercy of our Lord Jesus Christ to bring you to eternal life. Be merciful to those who doubt; save others by snatching them from the fire; to others show mercy, mixed with fear—hating even the clothing stained by corrupted flesh.

Doxology

To him who is able to keep you from stumbling and to present you before his glorious presence without fault and with great joy—to the only God our Savior be glory, majesty, power and authority, through Jesus Christ our Lord, before all ages, now and forevermore! Amen. (Jude 1:1–25 NIV)

Christ will come with legions of angels. I imagine the sixty-three million babies that Planned Parenthood has committed genocide on as being those angels.

The Church and the Titanic

On April 10, 1912, the popular belief was that the RMS *Titanic* was unsinkable. I imagine the conversation of the crew on the bridge moments after hitting the iceberg. "No, worries, Captain, it is just a little ice in the water. As we all know, the *Titanic* is unsinkable."

I am confident that conversation did not really happen, however, I do fear that a similar conversation has happened in churches across the world. There are people who believe that the church can weather the progressive's attack if they just compromise a little here and there.

The church is slogging along like the Titanic in icy waters.

Biblically, it's all good because it is supposed to happen before Christ returns. Please be warned, when Christ returns, it is not going to be pretty. If you are not in relationship with Christ, it is really going to suck for you! The organized church will fail. It is written. However, Christians will become even stronger than Satan. His minions cannot prevent this, but they will try to continue to divide us by race and origin to accomplish their satanic objectives.

Time for a Patton

The greater church is lacking leadership. At this point in history, the church needs a George S. Patton, not a wimp. The greater church is in crises from a socially driven issue to a true lack of scriptural clarity. Self-interest is the mantra of the day. Hurt feelings are of greater concern than spending eternity in hell for false teachings.

Abortion, of course, is my driving issue. I fear for any "church" that has taken the worldly stand that abortion is simply a woman's choice or health issue. Eternity is at stake! If leaders (men) were to step up and lead, where might we be?

8

They Fear Christian Men

History will show that one of the greatest lies ever told was that a baby is simply a choice. The second greatest lie ever told is that abortion is exclusively a woman's health issue. There is only one pregnancy that did not involve a man. That one involved the Holy Spirit!

Another lie is that men are not necessary. This is continually perpetuated by the willing accomplices within the media and entertainment industry. Consider how much effort Planned Parenthood and their co-conspirators have expended in removing men from the role of father and spiritual leader. It is not a mistake that they have tactfully removed men from being part of the conversation because if men are there and still having an ounce of masculinity, women of faith would walk away from the lies. Women, by God's design, are set up to be mothers and keepers of the home. This is not a sexist statement. It is in our very nature that women are far better at caregiving and nurturing.

So where have all the John Waynes or George S. Pattons gone? In a secular liberal world, men of character, integrity, and morality are passé, unnecessary, and, by all accounts, the cause of all that is wrong in the world, especially white men. However, black men are next. They will continue to do what they can to turn us against one another to accomplish their demonic goals. The militant female activist disdains mothers, housewives, homeschoolers, working moms, and especially women in a Christian-based marriage.

The demonic accomplices in the entertainment industry use their platform to propagate the narrative that men are useless. Just suffer through any half-hour sitcom and pay close attention to the commercials. It will become quickly obvious how incapable men are presented. We cannot drive, navigate, shop, take care of the children, cook, run a washing machine, or dress ourselves. Men, especially white men, are little more than moronic cave dwellers just around for comic effect and of no real meaningful purpose. It is presented that men are the cause of or have caused everything from repressing women, Asians, and blacks and are the leading cause of "global warming," if you buy into their collective insanity. It is all the work of Satan, and abortion is right in the middle of it. The secular world, academia, the media, Democrats and (RINO) Republicans, along with the entertainment industry especially loathe white men, however, they fear Christian men of all colors even more. Abortion has been a key part of their emasculation process. They present men as having no responsibility, and when faced with the choice of responsibility, men are cut off from the decision process, making them to be irresponsible and become the cannon fodder for their war against men.

Just as Satan fears the light of Christ and the truth in Jesus, the liberals fear men of God. Why? Because once a man surrenders to God's will, they no longer have power over him. Women instinctively will be attracted to those men. If I am wrong, then why is there so much effort to devalue the contributions of men, especially Christian men? Consider the difference of the men of the forties. These were real men who came home for dinner every evening, disciplined their children sometimes with a belt, and held the door for their wives at Sunday morning church. Now this is not to say these women were not just as important and equal in their respective contributions. Yes, times have changed, but again it is about being the men God desires rather than what the world wants.

Ten Percent of Our Grandfathers

If men of today were ten percent the men our grandfathers were, everything would change! To be more specific, I am referencing the

WWII generation that both of my grandfathers were part of. I lived next door to my mother's father who, because of smoking, had heart failure and Chronic obstructive pulmonary disease (COPD) that led to an early death. His influence was limited over me largely because of how ill he was. He died shortly before I had gotten my girlfriend pregnant. Had I been able to turn to him for guidance, I believe I would not have gone through with the abortion. My father's father was sadly separated from me in distance due to divorce.

In their respective generation, over sixteen million boys responded after the attack on Pearl Harbor. That was approximately eleven percent of the US population. The nation first placed our attention on Europe. In the end, the Holocaust was verification that we were fighting a war against a genocidal maniac who was responsible for the murder of roughly six million people. Meanwhile at this very moment, a genocide is occurring within the United States, primarily directed at the African American women. American men have yet to take on a genocide that has murdered over sixty-three million babies from 1973.

Imagine if ten percent of the men who only attend church on Christmas and Easter were to become weekly attendees and engage in the right-to-life battle, we would field an army of men that would rival the US Army of WWII (1941–1946). If ten percent of the total US population that self-identifies as Christians became weekly attendees, every pastor I know would likely be unable to contain themselves! However, if ten percent actually engaged and activated, the nation would turn on a dime, and it scares the hell out of the liberal progressives!

Planned Parenthood would be eliminated because the religious community could deal with unplanned pregnancies as it once did. Once politicians saw people in church again, they would have no choice but to improve their conduct because they would have a community within their respective districts they would be forced to answer to. That would scare the hell out of them and maybe put Jesus in them! Honestly, I have zero faith in politicians. I do, however, have faith in Jesus Christ. Men have been cast out of societal significance, and we only have ourselves to blame. The problem is, if we do not organize within a short period, we will lose all worth to earthly society.

Football

Yes, football! Time and again, I have heard the question asked, "How can so many men find the time, money, and energy to go to a football game yet cannot find the time to spend one and a half hours a week in church?"

My life began to change when a coworker asked me, "How do you expect to spend eternity in heaven when you're unwilling to give God an hour and a half a week?" The answer is quite simple. Men are hardwired for battle. Whether we admit it or not, we live vicariously through our teams. Each week, modern gladiators take to the field of battle. We watch it as though life hinges on the outcome.

Meanwhile, back at the church, the pews are empty. The church could be revived if, and only if, the church takes a hard stand of being the moral center and demonstrates that the men within the church are greater gladiators in the name of Christ than any man on the football field. Yep, I said it! It's not politically correct to make such an assertion; however, I flush political correctness every morning. In truth, the Bible is full of real men who are leaders of men. So how can I claim that real men are inside a church because it takes more courage to walk in the doors of a church, stand for truth, and trust in God than it takes to put on a football jersey and yell for your team. It takes a real man to admit there is something greater than oneself. It takes courage to accept your earthly flaws and persevere regardless. It requires a strength that only exists in the grace of God when facing a secular world while staying true to God's teaching.

My wife is a hockey fan, and I am embarrassed to sit with her at the games. This little five-foot two-inch blond bomb goes wild! It is hysterical to see my otherwise calm, conservative, Sunday school teacher jumping up and down over a puck being chased around the ice. *I am in so much trouble for sharing this.* My point is that battle is still battle. She would have been at the colosseum, yelling, "Send in the lions [not the football team], the furry ones with attitude!" Men and women love battle, it is in our DNA. God put it there by design. Although I cringe when my wife says, "I got hockey tickets," there is a bit of excitement as I get to see her out of her norm. Yes, it is arousing to me. I am a man after all. Yes, God made us sexual.

Another thing to consider, of the sixty-three million babies aborted just since 1973, what is the probability that the quarterback who would have taken your team to the Super Bowl five years in a row was one of the aborted babies? Just think for a minute about the likelihood that your aborted child might have been your colleges star! Have you ever just taken a moment to really consider what you paid for? Have you ever caught a glimpse of a little kid and just had that thought for a second. If you're honest, you know exactly what I am talking about!

God loves you more than I am capable of imparting. He is ready to forgive you so you can let go of the guilt and shame. However, you will be expected to be a new man, not the man the world has created. Relax, God expects you to be the man he wanted you to be. The difference is once you start your walk with Christ, he will polish the rough edges if you let him. You are not required to move across the world and be a missionary. Maybe you're calling will be to work with youth, do a building project on an Indian reservation, or work with the homeless.

Christ fields a big team. Just like a football team, not everyone is the quarterback! Yes, there is a water boy on Christ's team. If that is what you are called to be, then accept it. It will bring you joy that you cannot even begin to imagine.

As a public service announcement, I have just offended any secular liberal reading this. In response, I say, "Suck it up, cupcake! I am a man. God made me this way by his choice, and he made my wife into a woman any man would be lucky to be with.

> Lord, do not rebuke me in your anger or discipline me in your wrath. Have mercy on me, Lord, for I am faint; heal me, Lord, for my bones are in agony. My soul is in deep anguish. How

long, Lord, how long? Turn, Lord, and deliver me; save me because of your unfailing love. Among the dead no one proclaims your name. Who praises you from the grave? I am worn out from my groaning. All night long I flood my bed with weeping and drench my couch with tears. My eyes grow weak with sorrow; they fail because of all my foes. Away from me, all you who do evil, for the Lord has heard my weeping. The Lord has heard my cry for mercy; the Lord accepts my prayer. All my enemies will be overwhelmed with shame and anguish; they will turn back and suddenly be put to shame. (Psalm 6:1–10 NIV)

Let Me Spell It Out for You

Men, how many action movies have you watched and exclaimed, "I could do that!" or while watching every play of a football game armchair quarterbacking, you believe that if you were there, the outcome would be different. How many of us have stepped up and attempted the challenge of the military, firefighter, or law enforcement? Well, here is your opportunity to be part of something worth fighting for. Consider that the first special forces team were the twelve disciples. Jesus did not seek the educated, entertainers, or politicians. He knew they were useless. He sought men of substance.

The First Special Forces Team

- *Andrew (Peter's brother).* A fisherman; martyred
- *Bartholomew.* A missionary, might have been a royal; flayed alive with knives
- *James (son of Zebedee).* A fisherman; martyred
- *James (son of Alphaeus).* Martyred, his body was sawed into pieces

- *John.* A fisherman, died of old age
- *Judas Iscariot.* Traitor that betrayed Jesus for thirty pieces of silver; hung himself
- *Matthew.* Tax collector; speared to death
- *Jude (Thaddeus).* Missionary; killed by arrows
- *Peter (Simon).* Fisherman; crucified upside down on a cross
- *Philip.* Fisherman; died by hanging
- *Simon (the Canaanite, the Zealot).* revolutionary; died a martyr's death
- *Thomas.* speared to death

Christian men are the single greatest threat to the liberals, Satan, and the genocidal co-conspirators at Planned Parenthood. My personal focus is on the lie of abortion. Just as Satan fears the light of Christ, Planned Parenthood's greatest fear would be men taking responsibility for the actions they willfully took part in.

You are under attack! Do not take this lightly. As a man—regardless of color, height, weight, or political identity—you are the enemy of the progressives. The men that drink their kool-aid are simply useless idiots.

As a Christian man, you are the biggest threat to their lies. Real men would fight alongside those of us willing to challenge the lies. They are committing genocide on black America. Where is black leadership? They have enslaved themselves to the will of the progressive left. Money, power, and earthly position have brought them into an unholy alliance with the very people who intend to exterminate them! Each man who accepts Christ into his heart and life and starts a faith walk is essentially removing another seat off the secular crazy train! If you think they're nuts now, just imagine how crazy they'll go as men turn their back on their liberal agenda. When men turn to a life of integrity, morals, and faith in Christ, the world would change.

If you haven't noticed, I am speaking to all men!

When I say *man*, I am not speaking about the physical aspects of manhood because that is a genetic characteristic. I refer to being a man of God, regardless of physical stature, color, education, or sinful history. Giving yourself to God is freeing beyond earthly measures. It is eternal freedom. Just imagine Jesus Christ inviting you to be part of his team to fight the evils of abortion that his nemesis in Satan is using in a genocide even greater than that of the holocaust.

I will be the first to state that I have no desire to die as the original disciples did, however, I want to live for Christ with the same level of faith. So in my final moments, it can be said, "He died in the service of Christ!" My mission is abortion, a battle of good and evil. Abortion is *murder*. All lives matter from conception to natural death.

I pray that my message will reach as many of the sixty-three million men responsible for all the abortions from 1973 until now. Your mission may be to come alongside me in this battle, or it may be an entirely different mission to glorify God. However, it requires you stepping into the fight and standing for something—anything. Stop expecting others to do it for you. Christ has called you to be a disciple and to use your God-given talents to glorify God. This does not mean you have to give up living. On the contrary, becoming a man of God will prove to be the greatest journey of your life.

Men and Christianity are under attack. You can be part of challenging Satan, for your soul, your families, and your friends. Our country is being ripped apart by secularism, liberalism, and progressivism. They have successfully removed God from the schools and public discussion. They have removed men from the family, brushed aside in the abortion discussion, and excluded them from the raising of their children.

Imagine for a second that you are a member of the greatest special forces team to ever exist. Can you respond to the challenge? Are you really man enough to fight for something bigger than yourself? Are you worthy of being a member of God's special forces? You can be part of the greatest special forces team to exist as a warrior for Christ!

9

Where to Start

Most would suggest to start with the book of John, however, I recommend the book of Mark. Mark is no-nonsense. It spells out what happened in clear terms. Ask someone you know to guide you! Join a small group or Bible study. Just start.

In *What's Wrong with the World*, G. K. Chesterton wrote, "The Christian ideal has not been tried and found wanting. It has been found difficult; and left untried." If you have read this far, you have already done more than most. Now you are at a point not only to talk with a spiritual leader, but to make Christianity your identity, successfully live it, and help Christ make a difference in the world.

You being a Christian man can change our world!

Micah 6:8 provides a helpful framework for understanding what God requires of us and how we will bring about change in the world:

> He has shown you, O mortal, what is good. And what does the Lord require of you? To act justly and to love mercy and to walk humbly with your God. (Micah 6:8 NIV)

We must start with ourselves. You are called to walk humbly with God. You must have a plan for anchoring yourself spiritually. It is too big to do alone. Finding other men willing to step up will help you grow and keep you accountable.

Elie Wiesel tells the story of a Jewish man who set out to change the world. In his book, *Souls on Fire*, he notes, "Basing myself on the Talmudic saying that if all repented, the Messiah would come, I decided to do something about it. I was convinced I would be successful. But where was I to start? The world is so vast. I will start with the country I know best, my own. But my country is so very large. I'd better start with my town. But my town too is large. I had best start with my street. No, my home. No, my family. Never mind, I shall start with myself."

For myself, I needed to accept my responsibility in the abortion of my child, then change my attitude regarding abortion. It was one of the hardest things I have done—accepting the fact that I was complacent in killing my own child! I warn you, psychological mountains are often far greater than physical mountains. When I admitted to a trusted friend what I had done, he replied, "I would rather climb Mount Everest naked than face that!"

There have been occasions when I feel climbing Everest would have been easier! Becoming an anti-abortion speaker has taken me to an entirely different level. The first draft of my first speech was eviscerated by the people I asked to evaluate it. They said I was too preachy and would turn people away. It could have been easy to just give up, however, I knew God had called me to this mission. How could I deny God? So two things resulted: I have rewritten my speech at least twenty-five times and I joined Toastmasters. Now I have given many talks on the Walk to Emmaus weekends and gained basic skills. I accepted that to be effective, I needed to hone my craft. Now when I speak, the most common comment I receive is, "I had not thought of the effect on men." It is proof of the effectiveness of Planned Parenthood's lies regarding abortion.

When we try to change the world without firm roots in a relationship with God and a Christian community, we will fail. Our leader is Jesus Christ. The strength of Jesus (and ours) came from his relationship with God and close friends (his disciples). Between times of intense ministry, Jesus withdrew with his disciples to a secluded place to pray and share his concerns.

> Jesus went out as usual to the Mount of Olives, and his disciples followed him. On reaching the place, he said to them, "Pray that you will not fall into temptation." He withdrew about a stone's throw beyond them, knelt down, and prayed. (Luke 22:39–41 NIV)

Accountability is a key to success. I personally belong to three accountability groups! One is a Bible study, the second is with two of my spiritual guides (Jim and Ralph), and third is a large group that has met for over ten years every Saturday morning in a coffee shop. We share our experiences for the week and the challenges we faced. We also pray and exchange ideas to assist one another on the Christian journey.

Your most immediate opportunity for changing is sharing God's love in your relationships with other people—namely your wife, children, family members, colleagues, friends, neighbors, and acquaintances.

> Whoever serves me must follow me; and where I am, my servant also will be. My Father will honor the one who serves me. (John 12:26 NIV)

Your mission is to infuse your network of relationships with the grace of Christ, to show mercy and love in your everyday life. Consider the effect on your family and children when you step into the role of the spiritual leader of your family. Rather than sending your wife and kids to church, take them there, participate, engage, and be what God made you to be.

When I was single, if I had known how many really beautiful and real women where at church alone on Sunday morning, I would have been there. I am still a male! These are the type of women men should be seeking to marry! You might say, "If I knew then what I know now!" In my twenties, I was so lost spiritually. I kept pursuing the wrong type of women. I thought I might meet someone in a bar. Not to say it cannot happen, but, guys, I have seen churches where the girl-to-guy ratio is twenty to one! Now if you are going for the purpose of picking up women, please don't! However, if you really want to find godly women, a helpmate for life, and you desire an awesome life, then I have given you a key!

Please do not be like other men! Step up, be a real man, and lead your family. It saddens me to see the married women wrangling her kids on Sunday morning and seeing the sadness in her eyes because her husband isn't man enough to lead his family. Do not be that man-child. Make an inventory of your relationships: Who do you already know that is on their Christian path? Can you call on them to guide you and mentor you? Are there people on your list that need you to mentor them in prayer, study, or accountability group engagement? Who do you know that needs your encouragement? A kid at work, a coworker who is dealing with health issues? What a difference a genuine relationship would create. In the old days, we called it just talking to one another. Who needs what only you can do or give? *Your wife and kids!* Who needs to hear about Christ from you? *Your wife and kids!* Your attitude toward others will either open or close relationships as channels of grace. Again, being intentionally engaged with other men will keep you focused.

> So in everything, do to others what you would
> have them do to you, for this sums up the Law
> and the Prophets. (Matthew 7:12 NIV)

Do you affirm people or do you categorize people with labels? A judgmental attitude can be the greatest obstacle to spiritual growth. Do you fall victim to the lies of the liberal progressives and put people into groups? Classifying people in groups is the work of Satan. Do you see people for what they have been and condemn them to that or do you see them for who they can become and encourage them to rise to their potential? A new attitude can be an offering of love to another and well within your capabilities.

You need not be a biblical scholar to do this. Just be genuine!

Your prayers for others are acts of love. Through prayer, God can transform your relationships. Through prayer, you help others become changed persons and support them in their new life. Through prayer, God can open opportunities to reach out and witness to others the truth of a life in Christ.

> *Prayer, especially public prayer, has been a challenge for me so I fully understand the feeling of uneasiness about it. I remind myself that it is not about me, it is all about God. When I stand before him, I do not want to hear, "Oh, you were going to get in, except you never prayed out loud for me!"*

Years later, after I proclaimed and accepted Christ as my Savior, many friends came forward and shared that they had been praying for me for years! Your friendship with others is the means by which you can share your life and Christ. Remember this simple motto, "Make a friend, be a friend, introduce your friend to Christ."

Seek opportunities to share your relationship with Christ with friends. Expect them to be receptive. Be authentic in sharing your faith and display the difference your relationship with Christ makes. There is no right or wrong way to share your faith, only authentic and inauthentic ways. When friends make a commitment to Christ, encourage their new way of thinking and living through spiritual support, study of scripture, and involvement in church and meaningful ministries. *You are a man of God. He designed you for this!*

Taking it into Society

Then there is society. Without God, society can quickly fall to secular influences (Satan). God calls us to work for justice. Bringing Godly justice into the world will occur by building a strong network of Christian men. With God's guidance, earthly issues fall away. So how can you bring justice to the world, run for local office, especially the school board? Enjoy watching the progressives lose their minds as you influence the direction of educational programs that shall form the next generation. You are an integral part of the world, culture, groups, families, organizations, institutions, workplaces, and government. As a Christian, you can influence the direction of society based on how you participate within it. Christ has called you to transform your part of the world into a more Christ-centered, loving, and just world (society).

I am not suggesting you go at this like a hippie. Jesus knew there would be conflict so he instructed the disciples to arm them-selves! *Your* mission, if you are man enough to accept it, is to help Christ change your community by acting as an effective Christian influence in it. God calls you "to do justice, to love kindness [mercy] and to walk humbly with God" (Micah 6:8). This theme is evident in Jesus's plan.

> The Spirit of the Lord is on me, because he has anointed me to proclaim good news to the poor. He has sent me to proclaim freedom for the pris-oners and recovery of sight for the blind, to set the oppressed free, to proclaim the year of the Lord's favor. (Luke 4:18–19 NIV)

Identify situations of human need. There is a mission group a friend help establish called Get in the Car. They respond to the after-math of several hurricanes, floods, and tornadoes. As a man, when you see the aftermath of a hurricane, haven't you thought, *I could help those people.* Stop expecting that someone else will do it. You and I are the *someone else.*

Jesus identified such situations to which we are called to respond. He makes it clear how significant our response is. I experienced this shortly after becoming a Christian. On a Sunday morning, the pastor requested prayer for a mission team leaving the following week. One of the adult leaders injured his back so a replacement was needed.

Now as the pastor spoke, I was thinking, *That sounds like fun! I could build stuff, kind of like camp, stuff I love to do!* Meanwhile, my wife right next to me leans in and said, "You should go!" My hand went up so fast.

The following Saturday, I was headed to Kentucky to help lead a team of five teenage girls on several work projects. We faced many challenges. One challenge was working on a roof that was built on the side of the mountain with the gutter of the downhill side, being thirty-one feet above the ground. I measured it! I had to create a safety harness out of what I brought with me. I got to live out my inner MacGyver! Then there were the spiders, not your wimpy little ones. I had a conversation with one after it stood on four of its legs and showed me its fangs! I decided to duct-tape the girl's pant legs to ensure they would have no visitors while we loaded used roofing materials into a truck. They teased me, not knowing why I did it. When I told them why, they all hugged me.

To this day, when I see any of them some fifteen years later, the first thing I hear is, "Remember when you duct-taped our pants to keep the spiders out?" Then the girls decided that my tools all need to be named so my circular saw has been known as Betsy ever since! When I see it on my tool shelf, I smile with the memories of a week of living out God's plan. I share this to illustrate Christianity can be more fun than you likely think! Christ is pleased when we smile and when we find joy in helping others.

You can correct the situation. It is what men are designed to do, duct tape optional. Sometimes this means taking an unpopular stand. Trust me, being an outspoken anti-abortion man is not easy. However, I am inspired by God. I know where I am going so bring it on! Influence groups, organizations, and businesses where you can impart with Christian values. Challenge them to be partners on the road to a better world, not obstacles along the way.

Taking It into the World

I work a part-time job at a major outdoor store. The discount is amazing! When I started, the f-bomb was every other word! Over time, my coworkers gradually stopped using profanity. I get approached for prayer and spiritual guidance. Now this is three evenings a week. I used it as a ministry opportunity. I wear the cross I received on my Emmaus Walk. No one has challenged me on it! In truth, I was a little disappointed they haven't because I was prepared for battle! Wearing a cross means little, it is simply jewelry; however, if you are true in your faith, it becomes a badge of honor as well. It is a conversation starter.

You can start your mission within an existing group and learn from more seasoned Christians. As an example, you could volunteer at a food bank or soup kitchen or help provide food baskets to needy families during Thanksgiving, Christmas, or maybe spring break. I see people racing to downtown Detroit to serve at the Cass soup kitchen during Thanksgiving, yet when my wife and I took our youth group in April, the men were overwhelmed by our presence. Let the seasonal Christians work for the cameras and feel good on the holiday. Do something impressive and do it when no one is looking.

Maybe you are more suited to teaching people life skills that will help them for the rest of their lives. A pastor friend started an after-school program and utilized the retired engineers to teach students math skills. Whatever you choose, be a joyful witness for Christ in everything you do. Let people know by your actions, attitudes, and words that Christ is the source and strength of your zeal for a more Christ like, loving, and just world, that Christ is the *Way*. How are you called to be Christ like in your society? As Christian witnesses, we should exemplify tolerance and mutual understanding. In every case, Christ's spirit should be evident in what we do and how we do it. So how will you change the world? Jesus sends us into the world.

> One of those days Jesus went out to a mountainside to pray, and spent the night praying to God. When the morning came, he called his disciples to him and chose twelve of them, whom he also designated apostles. (Luke 6:12–13 NIV)

> Therefore go and make disciples of all nations, baptizing them in the name of the Father and

of the Son and of the Holy Spirit, and teaching
them to obey everything I have commanded you.
And surely I am with you always to the very end
of the age. (Matthew 28:19–20 NIV)

This field of ministry calls us to stretch our hearts, minds, and action. Start with finding a church that fits you. Learn, grow, engage in small groups, and seek opportunities to find your spiritual gifts. You will need a strong and firm foundation of faith, study, and action. Be the force multiplier of Jesus Christ. Drive the progressives further down the highway to hell they are on.

I work every day to honor God and thank him for putting the right people in my life to help me find the way. We need to be the men Christ wants us to be. We each have gifts, but please understand changing the world starts with one. Once you turn yourself over to him (Christ), you may be a blessing to thousands without ever knowing it.

10

The Only Easy Day Is Yesterday

In late fall of 1999, I was blind in one eye. My dad just died from an untreatable form of cancer, my wife left me, and I was selling timeshares! The only thing missing was a one-eyed, three-legged dog named Lucky. I just was not ready to give up my earthly ways yet.

I was convinced God had it in for me. I was mad at him because I felt betrayed. Although I did not have a relationship with him, I felt he owed it to me. That little voice kept whispering in my ear, "Why did you hate me? Why did you kill me? I was your child." The guilt and shame were there, eating me from within. Blaming him was easy. I mean, isn't that the modern way? No one is responsible for their own decisions or actions, right? I just continued to wander in darkness with an expectation of a miracle from a God I only knew in passing. If only I knew then what I know now! Is there a man among us who hasn't said that more than once? As angry as I was at God, God used my blindness to open my eyes! God is always with you. The question is, will you let him into your heart?

God placed two Godly men on my path who brought me a little closer to beginning my Christian walk. Although neither witnessed my transformation firsthand, they both preformed as God's disciples. First was Damian, a true Christian man. He was Jesus in the flesh. He saw something in me that I did not see in myself. Every day he came into the room confident in his faith. He was never shy about God's word or love. He would speak to me about Christ. He was never pushy, a Bible thumper, or at all offensive. He just stayed true to his faith. Through his spirit, I slowly began to open my eyes to what Christ had to offer. During the next few weeks, Damian was able to encourage me to a place where my mind and heart were opened. This led to me eventually accepting Christ into my heart.

One morning, Damian approached me and posed one simple question. He asked, "Do you believe in Jesus Christ?"

I was taken aback by this question. I didn't know how to reply. "Of course, I believe in Christ," I blurted out, probably for the first time in my life. Until Damian began the dialogue, I really had not given it much thought. I went about my business, looking for an opportunity to pick up the conversation.

Later, Damian approached me again and he resumed the conversation by saying, "Earlier you told me you believe in Jesus Christ. So do you believe that Christ died on the cross for your sins?"

"Uh, yeah, I guess. I believe he died for my sins!"

He just smiled and walked away. Now I was curious at what he was doing, and I really wanted to continue the conversation. An hour and a half later, Damian asked me again, "Earlier you told me you believe in Jesus Christ and you believe that he died on the cross for your sins, right?"

"Yes," I answered. "Why do you ask?"

Damian quickly replied, "So how is it you're unwilling to give him an hour and a half a week, yet expect to spend eternity in heaven with Jesus?"

I call that my "two-by-four to the head" moment.

The second Godly experience happened at a coffee shop where I frequent every morning. A young man named Rob, one of the baristas, saw the sadness when I made an offhanded comment pertaining to a scripture. Without missing a beat, he reached under the counter to pull out his Bible and then instructed me to go sit down. I was a bit shocked and did what he said. He started reading biblical verses. In truth, he overwhelmed me with his knowledge and ability to find the exact scripture that applied to where I was. He brought God's word to life for me and got me thinking. He closed by inviting me to attend church with him.

Unknown to Rob, after Damian had asked me how I expect to spend eternity in heaven, I began what turned into a fourteen-week odyssey of seeking out a church to fit into. I ended up attending over fourteen different churches until I found my first church home. By the time I attended Rob's, I had already been to twelve different churches. Sadly, here is where many churches have failed yet again. And what I experienced varied from one extreme to the other. At one church, I was told that I was not dressed appropriately. I am confident that God does not have a dress code; his focus is on our heart. There were several churches in which no one said a word to me before or after the service. Then, a few of the churches with greeters did the customary hello and handshake, and that was it. And of course, there were a couple of churches that went over-the-top of welcoming new guests to the point that I felt a little uncomfortable with the questions. At one church, an overly friendly guy keep touching my shoulder and asking me very personal questions. I left that church with the impression the touchy man was trying to ask me out on a date.

I decided it was time to try Rob's church. At least I would know one person. I waited in the parking lot until I saw him entering. Rob greeted me and immediately introduced me to people. What I noticed was that the people were closer to my age, and they seemed genuinely interested in where I was and willing to help me on my Christian path. In truth, what caught my attention was there were so many good-looking girls. I couldn't turn without seeing another gorgeous girl. I found my church…well, so I thought.

Then God did what he does best—he brought me exactly what I desired in a Christian woman! After my divorce, I began praying that this time, I was going to get it right. I knew I needed to start with a Christian woman. Within a very short time, I met a Christian woman, and she invited me to attend her church. I did not hesitate. Eventually, this woman became my wife, and we began our Christian journey together. And yes, I found my church home. What I discovered was that this church was what we needed at that point of our journey.

Damion had advised me to seek out a church that feels like my grandmother's house, a place of love and comfort. Do not make the mistake of going to a church because of what someone told you. Find out for yourself. I knew I needed God, however, I needed to learn and grow in my faith walk. If I felt uncomfortable, I would make excuses to not engage. It took fourteen weeks, nearly four months of every Sunday going to a new church. The path to a Christian life is not that easy and requires commitment and dedication to persevere, but it is well worth the effort. We are only talking about eternity here!

The bottom line is, God has gifted you. He has been calling you, he has wooed you, and he has been right at your door, waiting for you to open it. Still you make excuses about getting out of bed on Sunday morning. You are tired, you worked all week, you have other plans. Frankly, you are risking eternity. Begin the greatest, most fulfilling journey you can take if you allow Jesus Christ into your heart and leave the secular world to itself.

11

Right or Left, It Is Eternal

Dead flies putrefy the perfumer's ointment, And cause it to give off a foul odor; So does a little folly to one respected for wisdom and honor. A wise man's heart is at his right hand, But a fool's heart at his left. Even when a fool walks along the way, He lacks wisdom, And he shows everyone that he is a fool.

—Eccles. 10:1–3 NKJV

Jesus is apolitical, not interested or involved in politics. Why would he? He is above it all. He is the king of kings after all! Jesus is all about good and evil. The issue of abortion is of pure evil.

That said, look at some of the truths objectively in what we would consider earthly political matters. Secular, liberal, progressivism is no friend of God. Instead, they make the government or a cause their god (global warming). With God, the authoritarianism that the secular, liberal progressive seeks cannot exist.

For clarity, I consider myself a Conservative (really Libertarian), not a Republican. There is a difference. I have very little respect for the organized Republican party. It is no different than the Democrats. I especially have zero respect for politicians who are pro-choice and believe they have committed crimes against humanity, not much better than the Nazi war criminals. *It must also be stated, although I am a conservative in the world, my faith remains in Jesus, not in any government of man!*

Sadly, I think so many, especially the young, are no more than sheep, just saying things with little understanding of what they are standing for. I pick on far left modern Democrats more than most because of the absolute evil they advocate, especially with abortion. For this reason alone, I cannot support Democrats for anything greater than sewer attendance. Even that would be entrusting a demon of Satan to sewage and that may be too much trust.

The Can Is Open

Liberal progressivism is Satan's playground. A "Christian" that advocates for socialism is not biblically studied. God knew Ecclesiastes 10:2 hits the nail on the head, as does Matthew 25:31–36.

The Son of Man Will Judge the Nations

When the Son of Man comes in His glory, and all the holy angels with Him, then He will sit on the throne of His glory. All the nations will be gathered before Him, and He will separate them one from another, as a shepherd divides his sheep from the goats. And He will set the sheep on His right hand, but the goats on the left. Then the King will say to those on His right hand, "Come, you blessed of My Father, inherit the kingdom prepared for you from the foundation of the world: for I was hungry and you gave Me food; I was thirsty and you gave Me drink; I was a stranger and you took Me in; I was naked and you clothed Me; I was sick and you visited Me; I was in prison and you came to Me."

Then the righteous will answer Him, saying, "Lord, when did we see You hungry and feed You, or thirsty and give You drink? When did we see You a stranger and take You in, or naked and clothe You? Or when did we see You sick, or in prison, and come to You?" And the King will answer and say to them, "Assuredly, I say to you, inasmuch as you did it to one of the least of these My brethren, you did it to Me."

Then He will also say to those on the left hand, "Depart from Me, you cursed, into the everlasting fire prepared for the devil and his angels: for I was hungry and you gave Me no food; I was thirsty and you gave Me no drink; I was a stranger and you did not take Me in, naked and you did not clothe Me, sick and in prison and you did not visit Me."

Then they also will answer Him, saying, "Lord, when did we see You hungry or thirsty or a stranger or naked or sick or in prison, and did not minister to You?" Then He will answer them, saying, "Assuredly, I say to you, inasmuch as you did not do it to one of the least of these, you did not do it to Me." And these will go away into everlasting punishment, but the righteous into eternal life. (Matthew 25:31–46 NKJV)

Nowhere within the Bible does it state to turn to government for your needs. In *truth*, the Bible has more to do with freedom than anything else. Abortion is a deal breaker, erasing the names from God's book of life. Even if it is simply voting for a person that advocates the pro-choice position will not end well. I have had countless arguments with "Christian Democrats."

Christ called the disciples to help those in need. He says nothing about creating social service or governmental bureaucracy to address issues of the day. As you read beyond Matthew 25:36, you will discover that God is calling us to tend to the hungry! Politics is our earthly battlefield, and the liberal progressives are the enemy of God! They have conducted a genocide on the African American community, devalued men, and enslaved people to dependency. All fall into Satan's will in keeping people from God's love. Here again is where the church has failed by allowing the cancer of secularism to infect the church with false teachings.

I will state what others seem to fear saying. There is no God in socialism. The government cannot compete with God and the teachings of *free will*. Socialism cannot exist where there is free will and freedom. Abortion is right within this issue. It is one of the tools they have used not only to separate men from women, but to exterminate African Americans. Once you recognize that government is in opposition to God and his teachings, things become clearer! Why? Because government requires dependency to exist, and God threatens that because of truth.

So how can I state that far left modern Democrats are evil? Well, back to my cause of abortion. The Democrats have aligned themselves with genocidal policy orchestrated by a government-subsidized organization like Planned Parenthood. Yes, by design, they are targeting African Americans. The Democratic party is doing the work of Satan by funding the genocidal maniacs of Planned Parenthood. On this one issue alone, Democrats and those that support them are aligning with Satan and destroying the life God created.

Aligned with Satan

To be perfectly clear, I am stating that the modern Democrats, along with the middle of the road Republicans in name only (RINO) and a vast majority of politicians, have succumbed to the temptations of Satan.

> And the devil, who deceived them, was thrown into the lake of burning sulfur, where the beast and the false prophet had been thrown. They will be tormented day and night for ever and ever. (Revelation 20:10 NIV)

Killing babies is being applauded, and freedom is legislatively stolen. They identify with a party but, in truth, are only beholden to Satan. Why have they aligned with Satan? The simple answer is power, and they make it sexy. How could any self-respecting man advocate for the enslavement of people to government, advocate for the killing of unborn babies, and now the killing of live, fully formed babies or allow them to live long enough to harvest their organs? People must be made aware that these demonic forces are quietly passing legislation allowing for the euthanizing of the elderly population for convenience.

Satan has used earthly pleasures to separate people from God, and lies are his primary tool. From the moment Satan fell from heaven, he has manipulated the truth to create division, class warfare, and racial tensions.

Abortion Is Murder

Abortion is murder, yet in the progressive view, life is simply a choice that we as humans have the ability to decide the fate of. Since 1973, nearly sixty-three million babies have been sacrificed at the altar of convenience to Satan. In truth, it is a genocide!

The motivation to write this book is two fold: 1) the first was to wake men up to being men of God, not of the world and 2) motivate men to fight Satan.

Euthanasia

Euthanasia is another lie. Satan has manipulated people away from faith. Euthanasia is presented as a personal choice of free will when in truth it takes lives. The lie of Satan is that euthanasia is for the extreme situation where and when a person is suffering. However, it is in the fine print of every hospital admission. When you are asked if you have a do not resuscitate (DNR), it allows the hospital to save money and not expend resources. Yes, it is about cost. If the

Republican party had a backbone, they would be sharing this truth at every mic they came across. They frame it as a way to peacefully end the life for those suffering or the elderly who will not have a quality of life based again on earthly standards.

In 2002, the Netherlands legalized euthanasia. This has had devastating effects on their culture. In 2017, one in four deaths was by man's hand. The impact on families is immeasurable. People can now simply request a physician to prescribe the death drugs without any involvement or family opinion.

What concerns me is once we allow government to run healthcare, what safeguard will we have that the governmental bureaucrats might decide that certain conditions have a financial limitation set and once that number is met, an order is automatically generated to euthanize the patient? Satan smiles. If men stood up and followed God, and said *enough*, this would be over!

12

They Celebrate a Genocidal Maniac

Okay, I have been making allegations that those on the opposite side of the abortion debate are evil. I have attempted to explain that not a single abortion would be required without the involvement of a man, as biology requires. I have illustrated the failings of the church. I have given a simple outline of what can be done, but how dare I suggest that those who are pro-choice are evil?

Margaret Sanger Mass Murderer

Well, let the facts of who Margaret Sanger actually was reveal the truth. In this chapter, you will read a letter from the archives of Smith College where she spells out her intent to *exterminate* the Negro population.

So a simple question, why does the Democratic party fight so hard for an organization that has an expressed intent to exterminate black America? Why do black Democrats support Planned Parenthood and accuse anyone that speak out against it as being racist while the very organization they defend is established primarily in black communities, knowing it was intended to exterminate blacks? It is about power.

Here is the letter from the Margaret Sanger archives at Smith College:

December 10, 1939

Dr. C. J. Gamble
255 Adams Street,
Milton, Mass.

Dear Doctor Gamble,

It's good to know that you are recovering. I also am stepping up and have felt much better the past week.

Miss Delp was here for Thanksgiving, and I am more than delighted to learn that she was able to get $250.00 from the California Birth Control organization plus the $600.00 from the Federation. That's good; she is a go-getter and a live wire, very tactful and charming as well. I think that my pick of her has been justified, even though she is a little higher priced than the ordinary. She had been working on the article to be written by Miriam de Ford (Mrs. Maynard Shipley). They were good enough to send me a rough draft for comments and suggestions, and the important suggestion that I made was not to include Miss Delp's actual name in the article, because of the fact that her sister is married to one of the high spots in the Farm Security Department, and if the enemy started to work on her name, they might make it difficult along the line; otherwise I think the article is good.

As to my sending suggestions to the Federation: I think it is really unfair for me to do so. I am too far away to have the personal contact of the different reactions and it only holds up any definite project to have the pros and cons battered about which makes for more chaos and confusion.

Dr. C. J. Gamble
12-10-39

There is only one thing that I would like to be in touch with and that is the Negro Project of the South which, if the execution of the details remain in Miss Rose's hands, my suggestions will not be confusing because she knows the way my mind works.

Miss Rose sent me a copy of your letter of December 5th and I note that you doubt it worthwhile to employ a full time Negro physician. It seems to me from my experience where I have been in North Carolina, Georgia, Tennessee and Texas, that while the colored Negroes have great respect for white doctors they can get closer to their own members and more or less lay their cards on the table which means their ignorance, superstitions and doubts. They do not do this with the white people and if we can train the Negro doctor at the Clinic he can go among them with enthusiasm and with knowledge, which, I believe, will have far-reaching results among the colored people. His work in my opinion should be entirely with Negro profession and the nurse, hospital, social workers, as well as the County's white doctors. His success will depend upon his personality and his training by us.

The minister's work is also important and also he should be trained, perhaps by the Federation as to our ideals and the goal that we hope to reach. We do not want word to go out that we want to exterminate the Negro population and the minister is the man who can straighten out that idea if it ever occurs to any of their more rebellious members.

I agree with you that Miss Rose has done a remarkable job in thinking thru and planning the Project but she has worked on it for sometime. As soon as I knew there was the possibility of getting any money I put her at work drafting the plan for Mr. Lackner. She is excellent at just such a job. She hangs on to details, weaves and correlates them into the design. I shall never cease to have the utmost

Dr. C. J. Gamble
12-10-39

admiration and regard for her ability, and so far I have not seen anyone in the Federation who could take her place.

I am constantly delighted at the thought that you are getting better and now we must pray for Mrs. Timme who is seriously ill at the Doctors' Hospital in New York.

My regards to your Sarah and to yourself.

Sincerely yours,
MS/mh
Margaret Sanger

How can the Democrats (and some misguided republicans) align with Margaret Sanger and so openly embrace her hateful agenda? Either they believe it or they have no soul. What rational person cannot recognize that Margaret Sanger was just as evil as Adolf Hitler and one of Satan's own.

There is no other organization that is funded by the US tax-payer (You!) that uses those funds to then support candidates who will ultimately advocate for the murdering of unborn children than genocidal Planned Parenthood. Somehow Planned Parenthood has committed $45 million in supporting Democratic candidates for president in 2020. Keep in mind that this is indirectly your money via taxes being used to elect pro-choice candidates.

Here is an idea! Considering Planned Parenthood receives federal dollars and harvests baby organs for resale, I suggest a special tax on Planned Parenthood. Simply establish that Planned Parenthood should surrender $10,000 for every dollar they contribute to political campaigning at all levels, local, state, and federal. Additionally, there should be a ten-dollar tax for every dollar a worker personally contributes to political candidates. If it is discovered that money was funneled from Planned Parenthood to avoid campaign tax laws, the employee will then be taxed $10,000 per dollar donated.

Margaret Sanger was on a mission to exterminate black Americans! So either the Democrats are closet racists or the money is more important than truth. Either way, they are supporting the demonic act of sacrificing babies at the altar of convenience. In all fairness, the current Republican party is not much better as they struggle to figure out if they want to be on the Trump side of history or the progressive side.

Well, you might be under the impression I have it in for Democrats. Nothing could be further from the truth. I do have it in for secular liberals! They are anti-God. For me, that is reason enough to stand against their demonic intentions. They are not the same thing nor is a Democrat from 1960 the same as today's Democrat. Sadly, the Democratic party was hijacked by political correctness and '60s hippies!

The once great Democratic party of John F. Kennedy is no more. It is now filled with objectively some of the craziest people alive. They are the living proof we need term limits. I would even go as far as suggesting to repealing the Seventeenth Amendment. Returning to the original intent of the CONSTITUTION; ARTICLE 1 Section 3. (1) The Senate of the United States shall be composed of two

Senators from each State, chosen by the Legislature thereof (The State). That would help solve Senators from becoming fixtures of Washington, D.C.!

The Democrats have been wrong on history again and again.

- They founded the KKK.
- They were against the abolition of slavery.
- They were against the Trump tax cuts.
- They would accept the Mueller report until they wouldn't.
- They started the war in Vietnam.
- They are against boarder security.
- They started the department of education.
- The most egregious support of Planned Parenthood (baby murderers).
- They support ANTIFA (a domestic terrorist group).
- They support defunding the police! Need I really explain the abject insanity of that?

> *How many times must the Democratic party be wrong throughout history before people wake up?*

One of the most evil people lauded by the left is Lyndon Johnson, so here is some truth. President Johnson, then a senator from Texas, proposed the Johnson Amendment to the tax code that greatly restricted the free speech of pastors and churches on July 2, 1954 (Congressional Record, 9604). Senator Johnson's motivations, however, are much clearer. Around the time this amendment was introduced, Senator Johnson faced some political difficulties from organizations in his home state. Gary Cass noted in his book, *Gag Order*, "Senator Lyndon B. Johnson of Texas forced the amendment out of his anger that [two local] Texas nonprofit groups had supported his primary opponent." In an article titled "Why Churches Cannot Endorse or Oppose Political Candidates," James D. Davidson wrote, "The ban on church electioneering has nothing to do with the First Amendment or Jeffersonian principles of separation of church and state" (*Review of Religious Research*, Springer). It was prompted by

Johnson's desire to challenge McCarthyism, protect the liberal wing of the Democratic party in Texas, and win reelection.

Additionally, Senator Johnson tabled the Civil Rights Amendment in 1957 because he did not want Republican Dwight D. Eisenhower to have this victory. Anyone with an IQ larger than their shoes size should be able to see the similarities of the current Democrats and their obstructionist actions. How many lives were affected because of political motivations?

President Barack Obama delivered this address during the Civil Rights Summit at the Lyndon B. Johnson Presidential Library on April 10, 2014, "During his first 20 years in Congress, he opposed every civil rights bill that came up for a vote, once calling the push for federal legislation a farce and a shame."

> In 1947, after President Harry S Truman sent Congress proposals against lynching and segregation in interstate transportation, Johnson called the proposed civil rights program a "farce and a sham—an effort to set up a police state in the guise of liberty."

> In his 1948 speech in Austin kicking off his Senate campaign, Johnson declared he was against Truman's attempt to end the poll tax because, Johnson said, "it is the province of the state to run its own elections." Johnson also was against proposals against lynching "because the federal government," Johnson said, "has no more business enacting a law against one form of murder than against another."

Through the prism of history, this time will be looked at and the question will be asked, "What were they thinking? Were they thinking at all?" What is befuddling is how so-called progressive ideas have done nothing to enrich the greater black community. The only ones benefitting are the sellers of hate, lies, half-truths, and demonic objectives. The us-against-them attitude is again in Satan's wheelhouse.

"When we bleed, we all bleed red…and all of our internal organs are the same color," says Shelle (*A Woman's Cry*). There are only two real differences, first is pigment and the second is attitude.

Prior to the Great Society programs, the black family model was stronger than the traditional white families. In 1950, 17 percent of African American children lived at home with their mother but not their father. By 2010, that increased to 50 percent. In 1965, only 8 percent of childbirths in the black community occurred out of wedlock. In 2010, that figure was 41 percent. Today, children born out of wedlock in the black community sits at an astonishing 72 percent. The number of African American women married and living with their spouse was recorded as 53 percent in 1950. By 2010, it dropped to 25 percent. (The original report titled "The Negro Family: The Case for National Action" was released in 1965 by the late New York Senator, Daniel Moynihan.) Nearly 70 percent of black children are born to single-parent households.

Another lie is that Great Society will help people when it has been a tool in eliminating men from the equation. Another lie, the war on poverty will end poverty when more people have died as a direct result.

I have been called a racist, Nazi, homophobe, fat, bald, white, jerk, and the list goes on. Here is a reality check, I am a man of God. Jesus is my Lord and Savior, period. Label me if you must, but you will answer for it when you stand before God. I do not even hate the secular liberals. I think they are either brainwashed or mentally ill, but I do not hate them.

13

The American College of Pediatricians

The American College of Pediatricians concurs with the body of scientific evidence that human life begins at conception—fertilization...Scientific and medical discoveries over the past three decades have only verified and solidified this age-old truth. At the completion of the process of fertilization, the human creature emerges as a whole, genetically distinct, individuated zygotic living human organism, a member of the species homo sapiens, needing only the proper environment in order to grow and develop. The difference between the individual in its adult stage and in its zygotic stage is not one of personhood but of development. The Mission of the American College of Pediatricians is to enable all children to reach their optimal physical and emotional health and well-being from the moment of conception.

Conception

> While they were there, the time came for the baby to be born, and she gave birth to her firstborn, a son. She wrapped him in cloths and placed him in a manger, because there was no guest room available for them. (Luke 2:6–7 NIV)

Well, I truly believe human life begins at the moment of conception. Science has proven this to be true.

> In that fraction of a second when the chromosomes form pairs, the sex of the new child will be determined, hereditary characteristics received from each parent will be set, and a new life will have begun. (Kaluger, G. and Kaluger, M. 1974. *Human Development: The Span of Life*, p. 28–29)

> It is the penetration of the ovum by a spermatozoon and resultant mingling of the nuclear material each brings to the union that constitutes the culmination of the process of *fertilization* and marks the initiation of the life of a new individual. (Patten, Bradley M. 1968. *Human Embryology*, 3rd edition New York: McGraw Hill, p. 43)

Embryologists Ronan O'Rahilly and Fabiola Muller wrote, "Although life is a continuous process, fertilization is a critical landmark because, under ordinary circumstances, a new, genetically distinct human organism is thereby formed. (O'Rahilly and Muller. 1996. *Human Embryology and Teratology*, 2d ed., New York: Wiley-Liss).

Researchers at the Stanford University School of Medicine have shown that "they can predict with 93 percent certainty which fertilized eggs will make it to a critical developmental milestone and which will stall and die" (Stanford University Medical Center). To die first requires life!

Progressive Values

- Abortion, up to the moment of birth, is a choice, *yet the death penalty is immoral.*
- It is not rape if you are a Democratic leader (Bill Clinton).

- The accuser of a Republican is always telling the truth, regardless of evidence.
- Government can solve problems.
- Opinions are only welcome if you agree with the progressive.
- State-funded schools are for learning, so long as it is progressivism.
- Healthcare is too complicated an issue for doctors to figure out. It requires bureaucrats and lawyers.
- Some rich people obtained their wealth by stealing from the poor without sharing meaningful benefits or contributing to society.
- Moral integrity is a moving objective, especially when it concerns matters related to a Democrat committing a crime or ethical violation. If a Republican is questioned about morals, he is guilty of the crime that a Democrat would get a pass on.
- Everyone is equal (not really), but we'll lie to them because they are too stupid to figure it out.

Summary

History will show that one of the greatest lies ever told was that a baby is simply a choice! The second greatest lie ever told is that abortion is exclusively a woman's health issue. Lies are where Satan lives. Every abortion is a victory for Satan. Every time a man is removed from the decision or refused the opportunity to create a family, it is a victory for Satan, and it brings darkness to the world.

The abortion of my child was the worst choice of my life. The guilt and shame of that "choice" has negatively affected every aspect of my life. The weight of that abortion hung over me like an anvil, crushing my spirit.

Just as Satan fears the light of Christ and the truth in Jesus, the "pro-choice crowd" fear men of God. Why? Because once a man surrenders to God's will, Satan has no power over them. Those men will lead their families as God intended it. If I am wrong, then why is there so much effort to devalue the contributions of men and remove them from the discussion? Men need to realize that they have a voice in the abortion debate and need to be the men God always intended them to be.

14

Dearest Grace

Social media outlets provide the opportunity to share good news through connections, as well as misguided information. I have one more "good news" story to share. Through social media, I have been able to reconnect with Grace's mom. And after much prayer, I decided to send her a draft of this book as I felt it was important for her to know what has been on my heart—Grace! With her permission, I am sharing her letter that she wrote to me upon reading the book.

Dearest Spencer,

> *I am so very proud of you for writing this book. It is a huge gift to me to know how you feel. Thank you so much for sharing this with me. I have both goose bumps and tears. It's okay, though, it warms my heart, knowing you think of our child as much as I do. What you are doing is beautiful; the world needs more men like you! Thank you, Spencer!*

> *The abortion of our child was the most awful experience I have ever gone through. Trust me, the procedure of an abortion is haunting! An ugly awful, traumatic, painful, and emotionally horrible experience that never goes away!*

My self-esteem was destroyed, as well as causing a lifelong battle with nearly all the never-talked-about after-effects of abortion. I suffer from anxiety, smoking, endless remorse, and a sense of emptiness—all the postabortion effects no one ever talks about.

I held this inside me, putting on a smile, but crying internally. Trust me, it was the biggest mistake of my life. I am beyond proud of you for doing this. I love the name you gave our baby of Grace; it is so fitting.

I wish I could find the strength and ability to speak to young girls about abortion and the ugly lifelong effects! Trust me, the procedure of an abortion is traumatic and haunting!

I never would have known what you went through. You're right, no one ever talks about the effect on the man. I never had a clue you were struggling with the choice we made. I only wish we would have taken the time to actually talk rather than just react.

It is a gift from God you writing this book. Thank God, he pointed you to our guardian angel Grace!

Keep writing and speaking the truth! Although Grace is not here with us, she certainly is on our hearts, and I agree, our special guardian angel.

Sincerely, Grace's mom.

Dearest Grace,

Since I last wrote to you, God has put in my heart so much. I have grown closer to Christ and am continuing to fight for the unborn here on earth. I now can see with clarity God's hand in my life and the people he placed on my path to guide me home.

From 1996 to 1999, I was recounting how these years were my bottom. I now can laugh when I talk about how my wife left me, my dad died, and I went partially blind. The only thing missing was a three-legged, one-eyed dog named Lucky! However, I needed to experience those things to bring me to Christ. Although as I went through them, I cursed him. I see now how close he was, just waiting for me. The brilliance of God is beyond amazing! Throughout that time, I was broke financially, emotionally, and spiritually.

One ray of hope came with an opportunity to purchase a new bike. I was spending too much time wallowing in self-pity, watching the walls of my apartment close in on me. I jumped at it if only as an inexpensive way out of the house. It became what I now call pedal therapy. It was just me, you, and God. I just didn't realize he was along for the ride every day. I used my bike to escape all my issues. I rode it before and after work during weekdays and weekends, rain or shine. On one occasion, I started riding and talking to God (I thought I was just daydreaming) and rode so far, I had to call a friend to rescue me that evening when I realized I managed to travel over seventy miles from home.

God is so amazing. He will use our passions, our pain, and our troubles. We just need to look for him within the circumstances. He used my bike as a way to open a dialogue. I did not see it at the time, but those long rides gave me the peace I was seeking. On those long rides, the most important thing that came was my relationship with God. I started the process of coming to terms with what I had done to you. Although I still carry the remorse for what I did, the guilt and shame are gone through God's amazing grace.

My walk of faith has been a long one and will continue until I take my final breath. Before we meet in heaven, I will spend the remainder of my time here, enlightening every man and woman I can of how sinful abortion is. Christ has given me the scripture and the will to fight for you, along with the other unborn and aborted children. Satan hates me now because he knows he lost my soul on that April morning. I anticipate his demonic stooges will attack me and my character and use anything they can to destroy me. It is what they do.

Knowing that you are always with me gives me the peace to get through it. They can use their earthly ways, however, it's not earth that concerns me. It is being united with you in heaven for eternity.

God has so many tools, but sadly people fail to see the truth of God. Music is one of his greatest gifts. Unfortunately, it was not a talent he gave me. There are a few songs that bring me to tears of joy as my image of you appears the instance I hear them. I think of you dancing in the joy of it. Oh, how awesome it must be to hear a choir of angels singing in the presence of God.

Grace, I can say without reservation that God loves you, and so do I!

SCRIPTURE INDEX

Chapter 1

- *I thank Christ Jesus our Lord, who has given me strength, that he considered me trustworthy, appointing me to his service. Even though I was once a blasphemer and a persecutor and a violent man, I was shown mercy because I acted in ignorance and unbelief. The grace of our Lord was poured out on me abundantly, along with the faith and love that are in Christ Jesus. Here is a trustworthy saying that deserves full acceptance: Christ Jesus came into the world to save sinners—of whom I am the worst. But for that very reason I was shown mercy so that in me, the worst of sinners, Christ Jesus might display his immense patience as an example for those who would believe in him and receive eternal life. Now to the King eternal, immortal, invisible, the only God, be honor and glory for ever and ever. Amen.* (1 Tm 1:12–17 NIV)
- *Children are a heritage from the Lord, offspring a reward from him. Like arrows in the hands of a warrior are children born in one's youth. Blessed is the man whose quiver is full of them. They will not be put to shame when they contend with their opponents in court.* (Ps 127:3–5 NIV)
- *Since, then, we know what it is to fear the Lord, we try to persuade others. What we are is plain to God, and I hope it is also plain to your conscience. We are not trying to commend ourselves to you again but are giving you an opportunity to take pride in us, so that you can answer those who take pride in what is seen rather than in what is in the heart. If we are "out of our mind," as some say, it is for God; if we are in our*

right mind, it is for you. For Christ's love compels us, because we are convinced that one died for all, and therefore all died. And he died for all, that those who live should no longer live for themselves but for him who died for them and was raised again. So from now on we regard no one from a worldly point of view. Though we once regarded Christ in this way, we do so no longer. Therefore, if anyone is in Christ, the new creation has come: The old has gone, the new is here! All this is from God, who reconciled us to himself through Christ and gave us the ministry of reconciliation: that God was reconciling the world to himself in Christ, not counting people's sins against them. And he has committed to us the message of reconciliation. We are therefore Christ's ambassadors, as though God were making his appeal through us. We implore you on Christ's behalf: Be reconciled to God. God made him who had no sin to be sin for us, so that in him we might become the righteousness of God. (2 Cor 5:11–21 NIV)

Chapter 2

- *Therefore we also, since we are surrounded by so great a cloud of witnesses, let us lay aside every weight, and the sin which so easily ensnares us, and let us run with endurance the race that is set before us, looking unto Jesus, the author and finisher of our faith, who for the joy that was set before Him endured the cross, despising the shame, and has sat down at the right hand of the throne of God.* (Heb 12:1–2 NKJV)
- *"Not everyone who says to me, 'Lord, Lord,' will enter the kingdom of heaven, but only the one who does the will of my Father who is in heaven. Many will say to me on that day, 'Lord, Lord, did we not prophesy in your name and in your name drive out demons and in your name perform many miracles?' Then I will tell them plainly, 'I never knew you. Away from me, you evildoers!'"* (Mt 7:21–23 NIV)
- *He will punish those who do not know God and do not obey the gospel of our Lord Jesus. They will be punished with ever-*

lasting destruction and shut out from the presence of the Lord and from the glory of his might. (2 Thes 1:8–9 NIV)

Chapter 3

• *The Lord God planted a garden eastward in Eden, and there He put the man whom He had formed. And out of the ground the Lord God made every tree grow that is pleasant to the sight and good for food. The tree of life was also in the midst of the garden, and the tree of the knowledge of good and evil. Now a river went out of Eden to water the garden, and from there it parted and became four riverheads. The name of the first is Pishon; it is the one which skirts the whole land of Havilah, where there is gold. And the gold of that land is good. Bdellium and the onyx stone are there. The name of the second river is Gihon; it is the one which goes around the whole land of Cush. The name of the third river is Hiddekel; it is the one which goes toward the east of Assyria. The fourth river is the Euphrates. Then the Lord God took the man and put him in the garden of Eden to tend and keep it. And the Lord God commanded the man, saying, "Of every tree of the garden you may freely eat; but of the tree of the knowledge of good and evil you shall not eat, for in the day that you eat of it you shall surely die." And the Lord God said, "It is not good that man should be alone; I will make him a helper comparable to him." Out of the ground the Lord God formed every beast of the field and every bird of the air, and brought them to Adam to see what he would call them. And whatever Adam called each living creature, that was its name. So Adam gave names to all cattle, to the birds of the air, and to every beast of the field. But for Adam there was not found a helper comparable to him. And the Lord God caused a deep sleep to fall on Adam, and he slept; and He took one of his ribs, and closed up the flesh in its place. Then the rib which the Lord God had taken from man He [h]made into a woman, and He brought her to the man. And Adam said: "This is now bone of my bones And flesh of my flesh; She shall be called Woman, Because she was taken out of Man." Therefore a man shall leave his father and mother and be joined to his wife, and they shall become one flesh. And they were both naked, the man and his wife, and were not ashamed.* (Gn 2:8–25)

- *There are six things the Lord hates, seven that are detestable to him: haughty eyes, a lying tongue, hands that shed innocent blood, a heart that devises wicked schemes, feet that are quick to rush into evil, a false witness who pours out lies and a person who stirs up conflict in the community.* (Prv 6:16–19 NIV)

Chapter 4

- *Woe to those who call evil good and good evil, who put darkness for light and light for darkness, who put bitter for sweet and sweet for bitter.* (Is 5:20 NIV)
- *For God did not send his Son into the world to condemn the world, but that the world through Him might be saved. "He who believes in Him is not condemned; but he who does not believe is condemned already, because he has not believed in the name of the only begotten Son of God."* (Jn 3:17–18 NKJV)
- *But without faith it is impossible to please Him, for he who comes to God must believe that He is, and that He is a rewarder of those who diligently seek Him.* (Heb 11:6 NKJV)
- *Yet he does not leave the guilty unpunished; he punishes the children and their children for the sin of the parents to the third and fourth generation.* (Ex 34:7 NIV)

Chapter 5

- If my people, who are called by my name, will humble themselves and pray and seek my face and turn from their wicked ways, then I will hear from heaven, and I will forgive their sin and will heal their land. (2 Chr 7:14 NIV)
- *Then I saw a great white throne and Him who sat on it, from whose face the earth and the heaven fled away. And there was*

found no place for them. And I saw the dead, small and great, standing before God, and books were opened. And another book was opened, which is the Book of Life. And the dead were judged according to their works, by the things which were written in the books. The sea gave up the dead who were in it, and Death and Hades delivered up the dead who were in them. And they were judged, each one according to his works. Then Death and Hades were cast into the lake of fire. This is the second death. And anyone not found written in the Book of Life was cast into the lake of fire. (Rv 20:11–15 NKJV)

- *Woe to those who call evil good and good evil, who put darkness for light and light for darkness, who put bitter for sweet and sweet for bitter.* (Is 5:20 NIV)

- *But there were also false prophets among the people, just as there will be false teachers among you. They will secretly introduce destructive heresies, even denying the sovereign Lord who bought them—bringing swift destruction on themselves. Many will follow their depraved conduct and will bring the way of truth into disrepute. In their greed these teachers will exploit you with fabricated stories. Their condemnation has long been hanging over them, and their destruction has not been sleeping. For if God did not spare angels when they sinned, but sent them to hell, putting them in chains of darkness to be held for judgment; if he did not spare the ancient world when he brought the flood on its ungodly people, but protected Noah, a preacher of righteousness, and seven others; if he condemned the cities of Sodom and Gomorrah by burning them to ashes, and made them an example of what is going to happen to the ungodly; and if he rescued Lot, a righteous man, who was distressed by the depraved conduct of the lawless (for that righteous man, living among them day after day, was tormented in his righteous soul by the lawless deeds he saw and heard)—if this is so, then the Lord knows how to rescue the godly from trials and to hold the unrighteous for punishment on the day of judgment. This is especially true of those who follow the corrupt desire of the flesh and despise authority. Bold and arrogant, they are not afraid to heap abuse on celestial beings; yet even angels, although they are stronger and more powerful, do not heap abuse on such beings when bringing judgment on them from the Lord. But these people blaspheme in matters they do not understand. They are like unreasoning animals, creatures of instinct, born only to be caught and destroyed, and like animals they too will perish. They will be paid back with harm for the harm they have done. Their idea of pleasure is to carouse in broad daylight. They are blots and blemishes, reveling in their pleasures while they feast with you. With eyes full of adultery, they never stop sinning; they seduce the unstable; they are experts in greed—an accursed brood! They have left the straight way and wandered off to follow the way of Balaam son of Bezer, who loved the wages of wickedness. But he was rebuked for his wrongdoing by a donkey—an animal without speech—who spoke with a human voice and restrained the prophet's madness. These people are springs without water and mists driven by a storm. Blackest darkness is reserved for them. For they mouth empty, boastful words and, by appealing to the lustful desires of the flesh, they entice people who are just escaping from those who live in error. They promise them freedom, while they themselves are slaves of depravity—for "people are slaves to whatever has mastered them." If they have escaped the corruption of the world by knowing our Lord and Savior Jesus Christ and are again entangled in it and are overcome, they are worse off at the end than they were at the beginning. It would have been better for them not to have known the way of righteousness, than to have known it and then to turn their backs on the sacred command that was passed on to them. Of them the proverbs are true: "A dog returns to its vomit," and, "A sow that is washed returns to her wallowing in the mud."* (2 Pt 2:1–22 NIV)

Chapter 7

- *He will punish those who do not know God and do not obey the gospel of our Lord Jesus. They will be punished with ever-*

lasting destruction and shut out from the presence of the Lord and from the glory of his might. (2 Thes 1:8–9 NIV)

• *Jude, a servant of Jesus Christ and a brother of James. To those who have been called, who are loved in God the Father and kept for Jesus Christ: Mercy, peace and love be yours in abundance. Dear friends, although I was very eager to write to you about the salvation we share, I felt compelled to write and urge you to contend for the faith that was once for all entrusted to God's holy people. For certain individuals whose condemnation was written about[b] long ago have secretly slipped in among you. They are ungodly people, who pervert the grace of our God into a license for immorality and deny Jesus Christ our only Sovereign and Lord. Though you already know all this, I want to remind you that the Lord at one time delivered his people out of Egypt, but later destroyed those who did not believe. And the angels who did not keep their positions of authority but abandoned their proper dwelling—these he has kept in darkness, bound with everlasting chains for judgment on the great Day. In a similar way, Sodom and Gomorrah and the surrounding towns gave themselves up to sexual immorality and perversion. They serve as an example of those who suffer the punishment of eternal fire. In the very same way, on the strength of their dreams these ungodly people pollute their own bodies, reject authority and heap abuse on celestial beings. But even the archangel Michael, when he was disputing with the devil about the body of Moses, did not himself dare to condemn him for slander but said, "The Lord rebuke you!" Yet these people slander whatever they do not understand, and the very things they do understand by instinct—as irrational animals do—will destroy them. Woe to them! They have taken the way of Cain; they have rushed for profit into Balaam's error; they have been destroyed in Korah's rebellion. These people are blemishes at your love feasts, eating with you without the slightest qualm—shepherds who feed only themselves. They are clouds without rain, blown along by the wind; autumn trees, without fruit and uprooted—twice dead. They are wild waves of the sea, foaming up their shame; wandering stars, for whom blackest darkness has been reserved forever. Enoch, the seventh from Adam, prophesied about them: "See, the Lord is coming with thousands upon thousands of his holy ones to judge everyone, and to convict all of them of all the ungodly acts they have committed in their ungodliness, and of all the defiant words ungodly sinners have spoken against him." These people are grumblers and faultfinders; they follow their own evil desires; they boast about themselves and flatter others for their own advantage. But, dear friends, remember what the apostles of our Lord Jesus Christ foretold. They said to you, "In the last times there will be scoffers who will follow their own ungodly desires." These are the people who divide you, who follow mere natural instincts and do not have the Spirit. But you, dear friends, by building yourselves up in your most holy faith and praying in the Holy Spirit, keep yourselves in God's love as you wait for the mercy of our Lord Jesus Christ to bring you to eternal life. Be merciful to those who doubt; save others by snatching them from the fire; to others show mercy, mixed with fear—hating even the clothing stained by corrupted flesh. To him who is able to keep you from stumbling and to present you before his glorious presence without fault and with great joy—to the only God our Savior be glory, majesty, power and authority, through Jesus Christ our Lord, before all ages, now and forevermore! Amen.* (Jude 1:1–25 NIV)

Chapter 8

- *Lord, do not rebuke me in your anger or discipline me in your wrath. Have mercy on me, Lord, for I am faint; heal me, Lord, for my bones are in agony. My soul is in deep anguish. How long, Lord, how long? Turn, Lord, and deliver me; save me because of your unfailing love. Among the dead no one proclaims your name. Who praises you from the grave? I am worn out from my groaning. All night long I flood my bed with weeping and drench my couch with tears. My eyes grow weak with sorrow;*

they fail because of all my foes. Away from me, all you who do evil, for the Lord has heard my weeping. The Lord has heard my cry for mercy; the Lord accepts my prayer. All my enemies will be overwhelmed with shame and anguish; they will turn back and suddenly be put to shame. (Ps 6:1–10 NIV)

Chapter 9

- *He has shown you, O mortal, what is good. And what does the Lord require of you? To act justly and to love mercy and to walk humbly with your God.* (Mi 6:8 NIV)
- *Jesus went out as usual to the Mount of Olives, and his disciples followed him. On reaching the place, he said to them, "Pray that you will not fall into temptation." He withdrew about a stone's throw beyond them, knelt down and prayed.* (Lk 22:39–41 NIV)
- *Whoever serves me must follow me; and where I am, my servant also will be. My Father will honor the one who serves me.* (Jn 12:26 NIV)
- *So in everything, do to others what you would have them do to you, for this sums up the Law and the Prophets.* (Mt 7:12 NIV)
- *The spirit of the Lord is on me, because he has anointed me to proclaim good news to the poor. He has sent me to proclaim freedom for the prisoners and recovery of sight for the blind, to set the oppressed free, to proclaim the year of the Lord's favor.* (Lk 4:18–19 NIV)
- *One of those days Jesus went out to a mountainside to pray, and spent the night praying to God. When the morning came, he called his disciples to him and chose twelve of them, whom he also designated apostles.* (Lk 6:12–13 NIV)
- *Therefore go and make disciples of all nations, baptizing them in the name of the Father and of the Son and of the Holy Spirit, and teaching them to obey everything I have commanded you. And surely I am with you always to the very end of the age.* (Mt 28:19–20 NIV)

Chapter 11

- *Dead flies putrefy the perfumer's ointment, And cause it to give off a foul odor; So does a little folly to one respected for wisdom and honor. A wise man's heart is at his right hand, But a fool's heart at his left. Even when a fool walks along the way, He lacks wisdom, And he shows everyone that he is a fool.* (Eccl 10:1–3 NKJV)
- *"When the Son of Man comes in His glory, and all the holy angels with Him, then He will sit on the throne of His glory. All the nations will be gathered before Him, and He will separate them one from another, as a shepherd divides his sheep from the goats. And He will set the sheep on His right hand, but the goats on the left. Then the King will say to those on His right hand, 'Come, you blessed of My Father, inherit the kingdom prepared for you from the foundation of the world: for I was hungry and you gave Me food; I was thirsty and you gave Me drink; I was a stranger and you took Me in; I was naked and you clothed Me; I was sick and you visited Me; I was in prison and you came to Me.' Then the righteous will answer Him, saying, 'Lord, when did we see You hungry and feed You, or thirsty and give You drink? When did we see You a stranger and take You in, or naked and clothe You? Or when did we see You sick, or in prison, and come to You?' And the King will answer and say to them, 'Assuredly, I say to you, inasmuch as you did it to one of the least of these My brethren, you did it to Me.' Then He will also say to those on the left hand, 'Depart from Me, you cursed, into the everlasting fire prepared for the devil and his angels: for I was hungry and you gave Me no food; I was thirsty and you gave Me no drink; I was a stranger and you did not take Me in, naked and you did not clothe Me, sick and in prison and you did not visit Me.' Then they also will answer Him, saying, 'Lord, when did we see You hungry or thirsty or a stranger or naked or sick or in prison, and did not minister to You?' Then He will answer them, saying, 'Assuredly, I say to you, inasmuch as you did not do it to one*

of the least of these, you did not do it *to Me.' And these will go away into everlasting punishment, but the righteous into eternal life."* (Mt 25:31–46 NKJV)

- *And the devil, who deceived them, was thrown into the lake of burning sulfur, where the beast and the false prophet had been thrown. They will be tormented day and night for ever and ever.* (Rv 20:10 NIV)

Chapter 12

- *There are six things the Lord hates, seven that are detestable to him: haughty eyes, a lying*
- *tongue, hands that shed innocent blood, a heart that devises wicked schemes, feet that are quick to rush into evil, a false witness who pours out lies and a person who stirs up conflict in the community. (Proverbs 6:16)*

Chapter 13

- *While they were there, the time came for the baby to be born, and she gave birth to her firstborn, a son. She wrapped him in cloths and placed him in a manger, because there was no guest room available for them.* (Lk 2:6–7 NIV)

REFERENCES

Al et, Lega. 2019. "study titled Maternal Suicide in Italy" published in the journal Archives of Women's Mental Health. PubMed. gov, Springer. Berlin.

Baker, John (Edited by) 2016. NIV Celebrate Recovery Study Bible. Published by Zondervan, Grand Rapids, Michigan, USA.

Brokaw, Tom. 1998. *The Greatest Generation*. Random House, New York, NY, USA. ISBN 9781400063147.

Carnegie Collection of Embryology, visualized at Virtual Human Embryo., www.prenatalorigins.org/virtual-human-embryo.

Carnegie Stages of Early Human Embryonic Development.

Cass, Gary. 2005 Gag Order. Xulon Press Fairfax, VA, USA.

CBS News. 2017. Euthanasia Deaths Becoming Common in Netherlands. Associated Press, London, United Kingdom, UK.

Chesterton, G. K. 1910. *Chesterton What's Wrong with the World*. Cassell and Company Limited, London, United Kingdom, UK.

Congressional Records Library of Congress. Washington, D.C., USA.

https://2019.michiganumc.org. *Daily News*. 2019 "A Daily Summary of Annual Conference and Look at the Day Ahead." Michigan Conference Center, Lansing, Michigan, USA.

Davidson, James D. 1998. Why Churches Cannot Endorse or Oppose Political Candidates, "Review of Religious Research," Vol. 40 No. 1 Purdue University. Published by Springer, New York, New York, USA.

democrats.org. DEMOCRATIC NATIONAL COMMITTEE Washington DC., USSR.

Gissler, M., et. al. 2005. "Injury Deaths, Suicides, and Homicides Associated with Pregnancy, Finland 1987–2000." *European J.*

Public Health 15, no. (5): 459–63 (2005). Published by Oxford University Press on behalf of the European Public Health Association. Finland.

Gissler, M., et. al.—2004. "Methods for Identifying Pregnancy-Associated Deaths: Population-Based Data from Finland 1987–2000." *Paediatr Perinat Epidemiol* 18, no. (6): 448–55 (2004). Published by Oxford University Press on behalf of the European Public Health Association. Finland.

Gissler, M., et. al.—1997. "Pregnancy Associated Deaths in Finland 1987–1994:—Definition Problems and Benefits of Record Linkage." *Acta Obsetricia et Gynecologica Scandinavica* 76, 651–657 (1997). Published by Oxford University Press on behalf of the European Public Health Association. Finland.

Goebbels, Joseph. 1931. "Goebbels on the Power of Propaganda." by Joseph Goebbels. Required reading for members of the media and DNC. Berlin, Germany, EU.

gop.com. Washington, D.C., USA.

Kaluger, G., and Kaluger, M., 1974. *Human Development: The Span of Life*. Page 28–29. Times Mirror/Mosby College Publishing, St. Louis, MO, USA. 1984, ISBN 9780801626135.

Kahlenborn, Dr. Chris. 2001. *Breast Cancer: Its Link to Abortion and the Birth Control Pill.* Published by One More Soul, Dayton, OH, USA.
ISBN-13: 978-0966977738.
ISBN-10: 0-9669777-3-4.

LifeNews.com.

Margaret Sanger archives at Smith College, December 10, 1939. Letter to Dr. C. J. Gamble, explaining plan to exterminate the Negro population. Archives is of Smith College, Northampton, Massachusetts, USA.

Mattera, Bishop Joseph G. 2014. ChrarismaNews 8 "Clear Signs of a Compromising Church." Charisma News 8, Lake Mary, FL, USA.

McCann, Steve. 2019. "Democrats, the Media, and the Big Lie." Publisher the American Thinker. El Cerrito, CA, USA.

Moynihan, Daniel Patrick "Pat". 1965. "The Negro Family: The Case for National Action." Published by Cosimo Books New York, NY, USA.
ISBN 978-1-945934-29-2.

National Right to Life News. 2013. "Abortion and Suicide: The Grim Statistics." National Right to Life News Alexandria, VA, USA.

Obama, President Barack. 2014. Address Civil Rights Summit at the Lyndon B. Johnson Presidential Library. Austin, TX, USA.

Odya Erin, Maggie A. Norris. 2017 Anatomy and Physiology for Dummies. Wiley Brand. Hoboken, NJ, USA.
ISBN 9781119345237

O'Rahilly and Muller. 1996. Human Embryology and Teratology, 2nd ed., Wiley-Liss; 2nd Edition (May 11, 1996) New York, NY, USA.
ISBN 9780471133513

Patten, Bradley M. 1968. Human Embryology, 3rd edition. Published by McGraw Hill Book Company, New York, NY, USA.

Patton Jr., George S. 1947. War as I Knew It: The Great Commanders. Houghton Mifflin Co. Boston, MA, USA.
ISBN-13: 9781125510919

Pera, Renee Reijo PhD. 2010. "Earlier, More Accurate Prediction of Embryo Survival Enabled by Research," p. 1–3., Publisher by Stanford Medicine News Center, Stanford, CA.

Reardon, DC et. al. 1, Philip G Ney, Fritz Scheuren, Jesse Cougle, Priscilla K Coleman, Thomas W Strahan 2002., "Deaths Associated With Pregnancy Outcome: A Record Linkage Study of Low Income Women.," Southern Medical Journal 95, no. (8):834-41. SIEC No: 20030262. Birmingham, AL, USA.

Review of Religious Research. 1971. The Official Journal of the Religious Research Association Volume 10. Machynlleth, Powys, Wales, United Kingdom.

Roe v. Wade. 1973. 410 U.S. 113 No. 70–18 (US Supreme Court 1973). Argued December 13, 1971. Reargued October 11, 1972. Decided January 22, 1973, 410 U.S. 113 US Supreme Court. Washington, D.C., USA.

Shelle. 2012. A Woman's Cry. Published by AuthorHouse, Bloomington, IN, USA.
ISBN-13: 9781477212202
ISBN-10: 1477212205

Stanford News and Medicine. 2010. Carnegie Stages of Early Human Embryonic Development. Carnegie Collection of Embryology, visualized at Virtual Human Embryo. Published by Stanford News and Medicine. Stanford, CA.

Stanford News and Medicine.—(2010). "Earlier, More Accurate Prediction of Embryo Survival Enabled by Research," p. 1–3., Available at med.stanford.edumed.stanford.edu. Published by Stanford News and Medicine. Stanford, CA.

TheBMJ.com. 1996. "Suicides After Pregnancy in Finland, 1987–94: Register Linkage Study." BMJ 1996; 313.

The Holy Bible: NIV, NKJV, and KJV versions.

US Constitution. 1787. Philadelphia, PA

Library of Congress, Washington D.C., USA.

Wiesel, Elie, Alfred Alvarez. 1972. Souls on Fire: Portraits and Legends of Hasidic Masters. Simon & Schuster, New York, NY, USA.
ISBN-13: 9780671441715
ISBN-10: 067144171X

Additional Resources

ABOUT THE AUTHOR

G. Spencer Schirs was born and raised in Michigan. After his parents' divorce, he moved with his mom and sister to a small town on the westside of the state. It was there where he began a rebellious adventure. Although he was baptized and attended church, he did not experience having Jesus in his heart until later in his journey.

As a teenager, he found himself in a difficult situation of a teenage pregnancy. His choice was to take the easy route and pay for an abortion. Problem solved, so he thought, and he moved on. Spencer is also a diabetic, and his lifestyle did not align with the doctors recommendations.

As a result of many poor choices, he woke up blind in 1996 and had to endure multiple eye surgeries. At the same time, Spencer watched his father die from an untreatable form of cancer, and his first marriage fall apart. The anger and turmoil inside his heart led him to contemplating suicide. At one of his doctor's appointments, he heard the doctor share how he was amazed with another patient who had no more than three months to live, yet he was still fighting every minute of every day. Without realizing it at the time, God was working on Spencer by placing key people into his life that impacted his heart, opening the door for Christ to enter.

Through the help of colleagues and friends, Spencer began the journey of building his relationship with his heavenly Father. It was not easy, and there were times he just wanted to give up. In 2005, Spencer had the opportunity to attend a Christian retreat. During this weekend, Spencer experienced the agape love and grace of God. His heart and eyes were finally opened.

Although Spencer was able to feel the forgiveness of God, he knew he had to do more. He actively promotes Right to Life of

Michigan and Pro-Life causes. He continues to share his testimony of the emotional effect of abortion on men.

His Christian walk continues to grow, and he remains open to where God would like to use him, praying daily to focus on Gods plan, not his own. Spencer has been active within the SEM Emmaus community, local church outreach programs for the homeless, leading youth groups, and men's accountability groups. Spencer believes the church needs to do more and respond to the issues of abortion, family, and race. The church cannot do this alone.

Whether he speaks to one or one thousand, Spencer's mission is to share how God's love and truth through scripture can impart that it is never too late to follow Jesus and be the person God intended us to be!